Every Light That Shines at Christmas

Ernie Haase & Signature Sound

Songbook

Musical Arrangements by Wayne Haun
Music Transcriptions and Engraving by David McDonald
Kimberly Meiste, Editor
Graphic Design: Brad Strider, Tribute Media Source

lillenas
PUBLISHING COMPANY

Copyright © 2009 by Ernie Haase & Signature Sound. All rights reserved.

Contents

All I Want Is You	84
Amen	107
Changed by a Baby Boy	39
Christmas in Indiana	91
Christmas Is Christmas (Wherever You Are)	62
Every Light That Shines at Christmas	23
God Rest Ye Merry Gentlemen	67
He Started the Whole World Singing *with* O Come, All Ye Faithful	5
If It Doesn't Snow on Christmas	77
Light a Candle	98
Marshmallow World	15
Mr. Heat Miser	48
Redeeming Love	33
Silent Night	97
Thank God for Kids	56
What Child Is This?	70

He Started the Whole World Singing

with
O Come, Let Us Adore Him

GLORIA GAITHER

WILLIAM J. GAITHER
and CHRIS WATERS

Copyright © 1982 and this arr © 2009 Gaither Music Company/ASCAP (All rights controlled by Gaither Music Company)/
EMI Blackwood Music, Inc. /BMI. International copyrights secured. All rights reserved. Used by permission.

PLEASE NOTE: Copying of this product is NOT covered by CCLI licenses. For CCLI information call 1-800-234-2446.

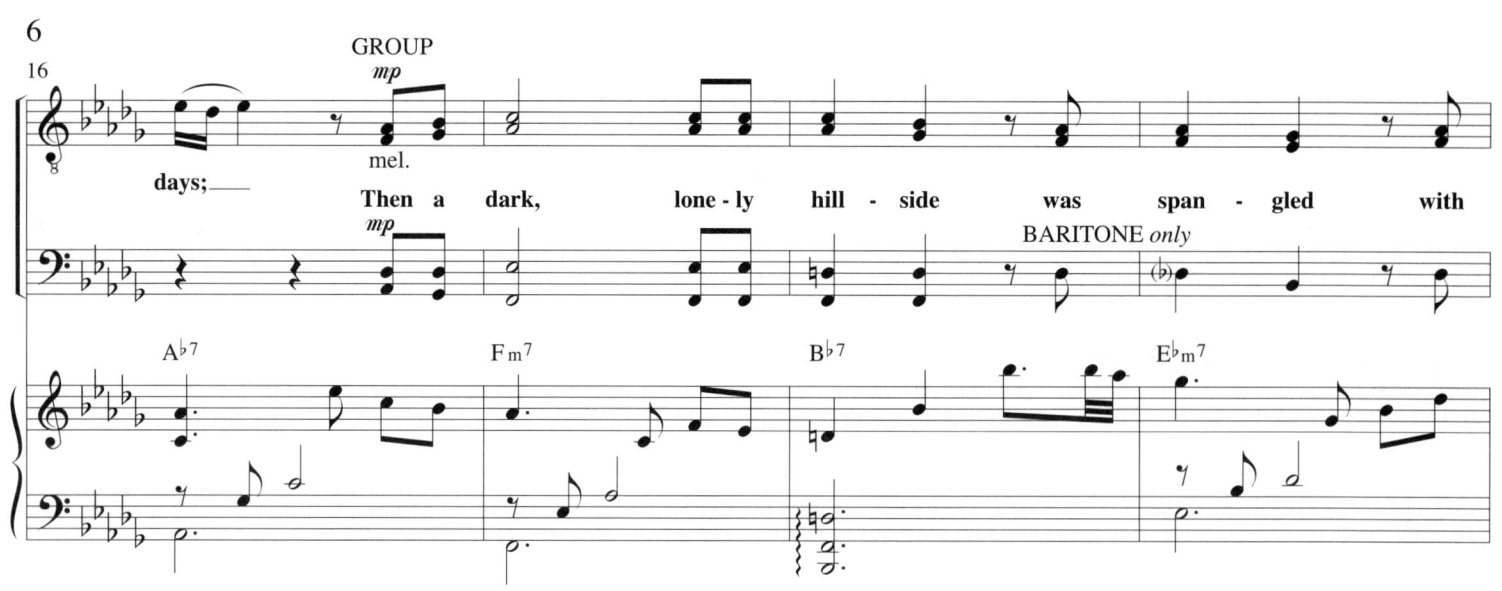

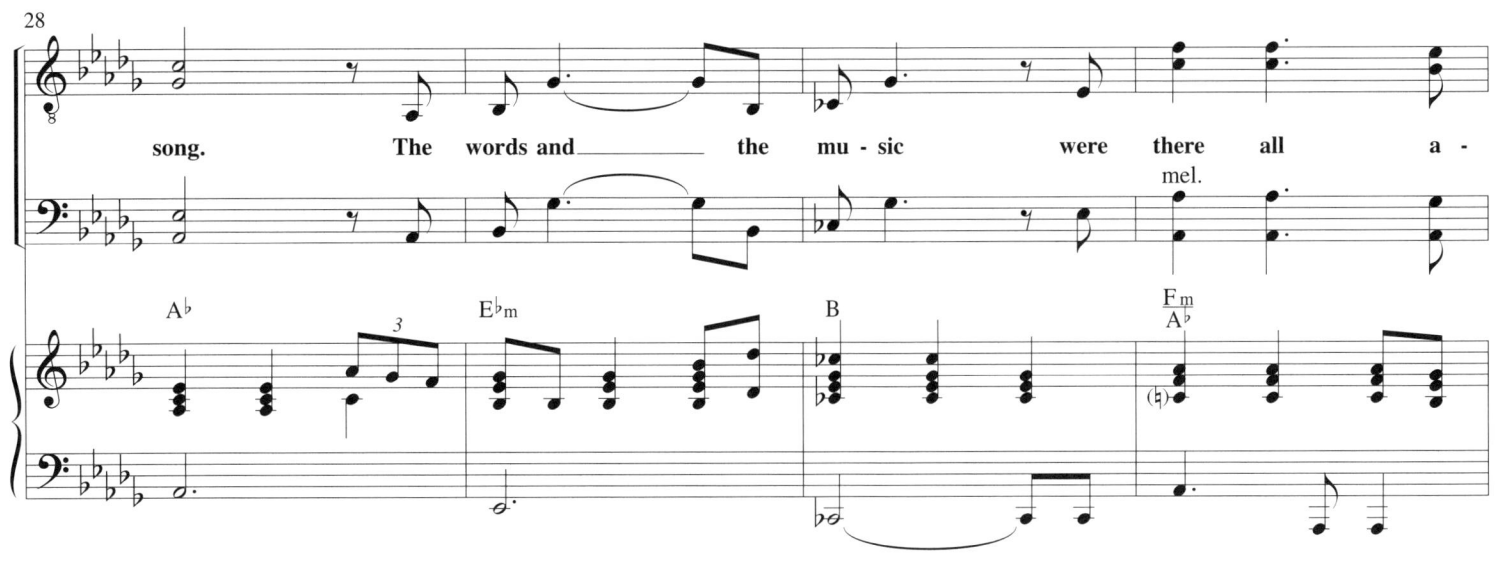
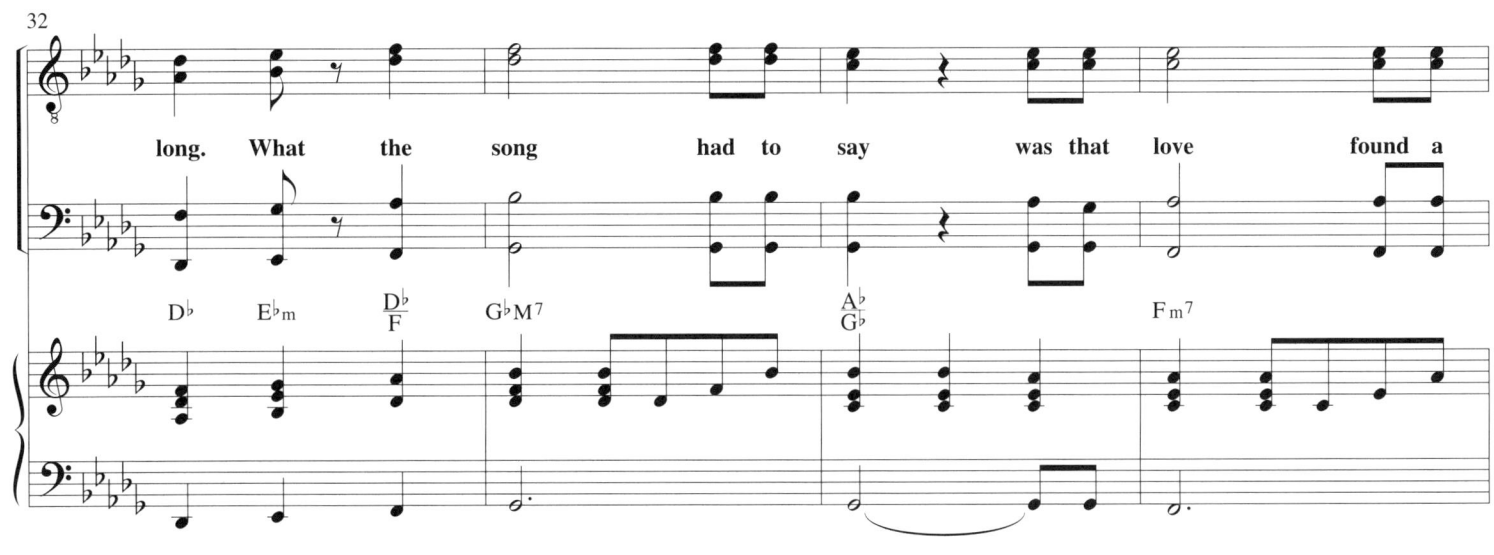

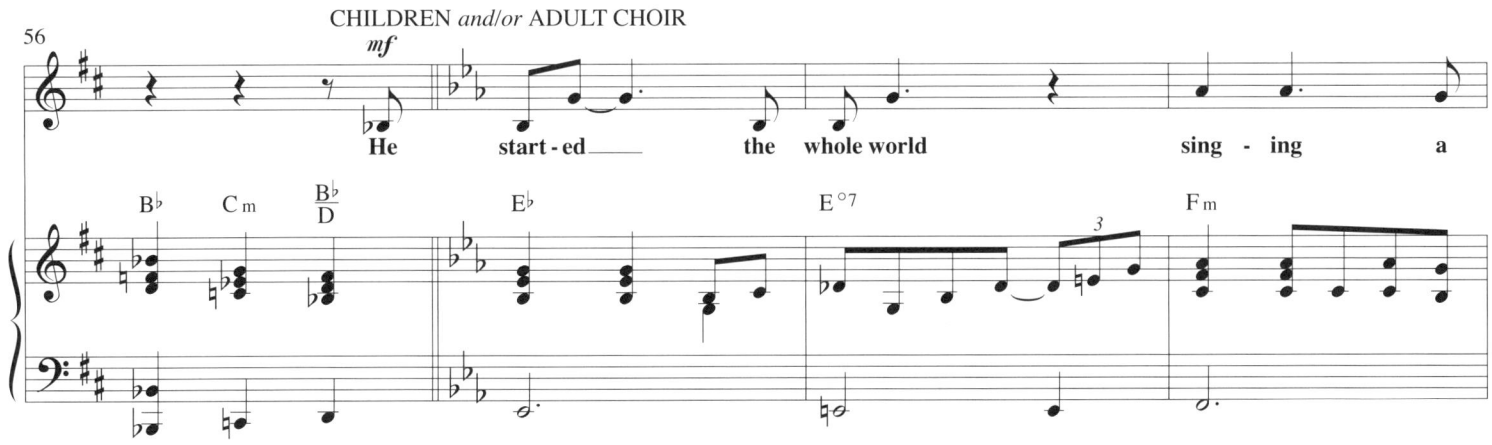
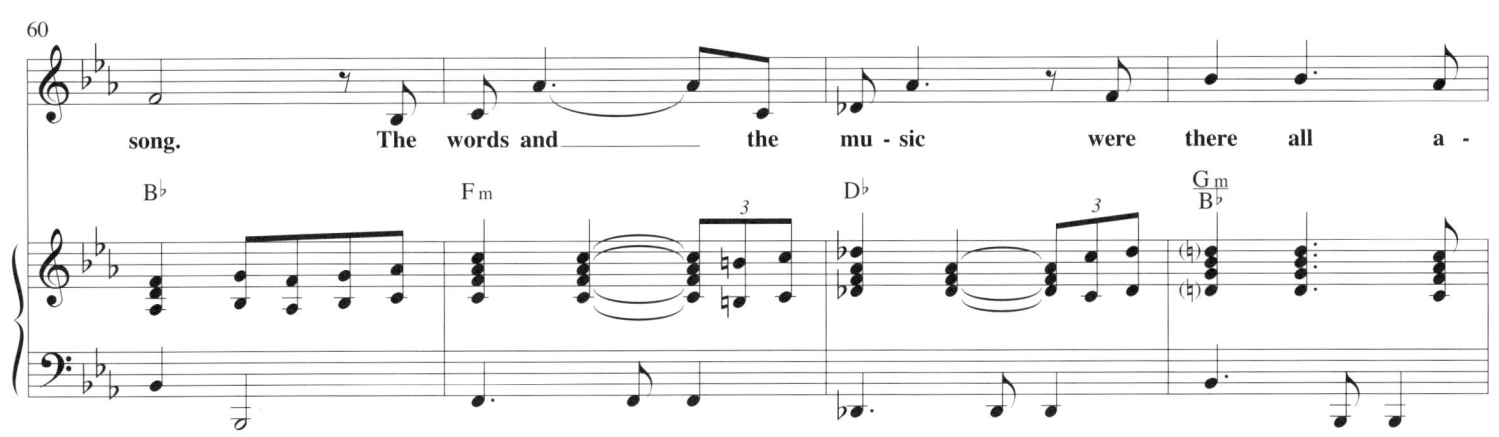

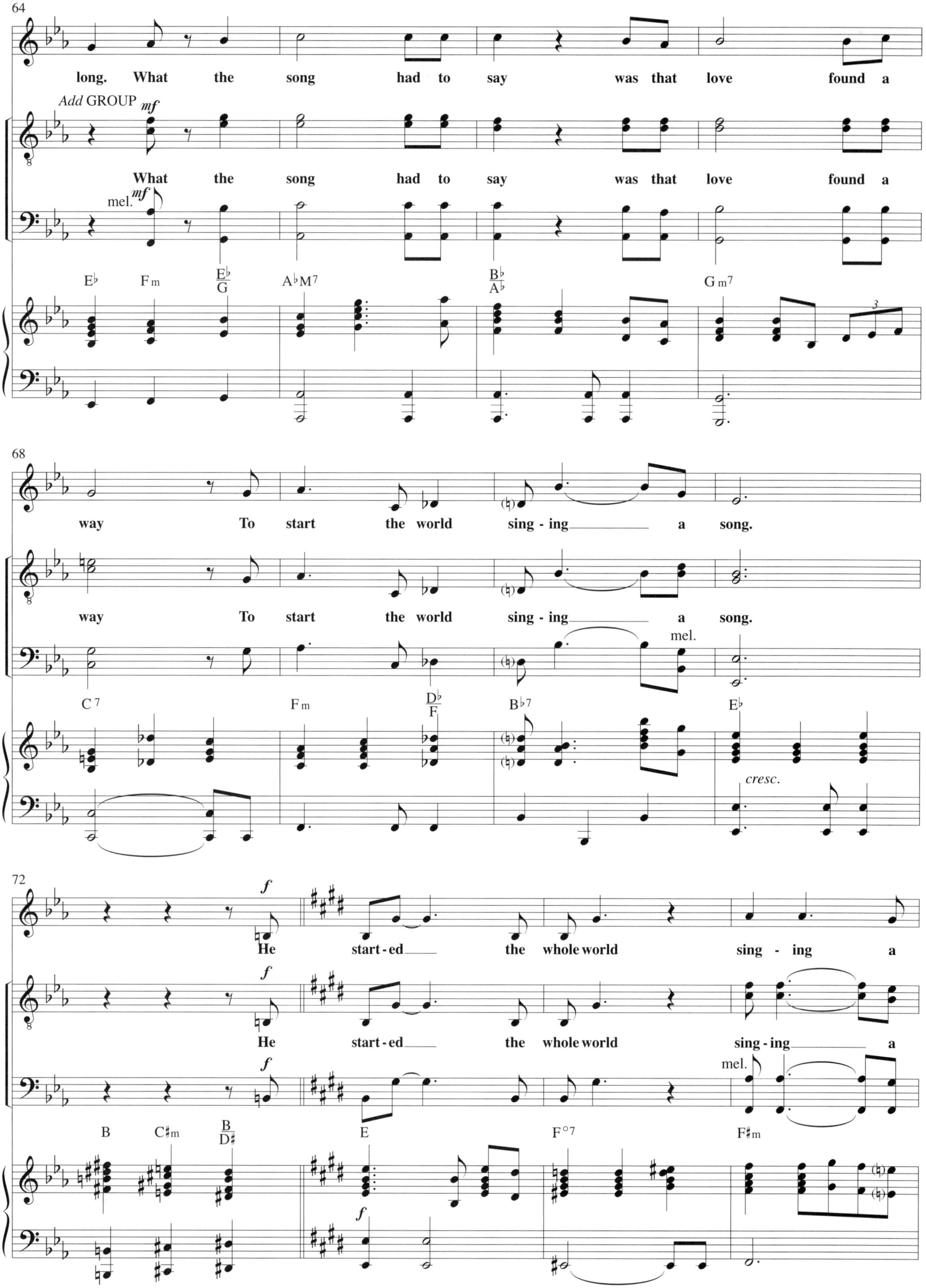
64
long. What the song had to say was that love found a
Add GROUP mf
What the song had to say was that love found a
mel. mf
E♭ Fm E♭/G A♭M7 B♭/A♭ Gm7
3
68
way To start the world sing - ing a song.
way To start the world sing - ing a song.
mel.
C7 Fm D♭/F B♭7 E♭
cresc.
72
f
He start - ed the whole world sing - ing a
f
He start - ed the whole world sing - ing a
f
mel.
B C♯m B/D♯ E F°7 F♯m
f

Marshmallow World

CARL SIGMAN
PETER DEROSE

Copyright © 1949, 1950 (Renewed) and this arr. © 2009 by Music Sales Corporation and Shapiro,
Bernstein & Co., Inc., New York/ASCAP. International copyrights secured.
All rights reserved. Used by permission.

PLEASE NOTE: Copying of this product is NOT covered by CCLI licenses. For CCLI information call 1-800-234-2446.

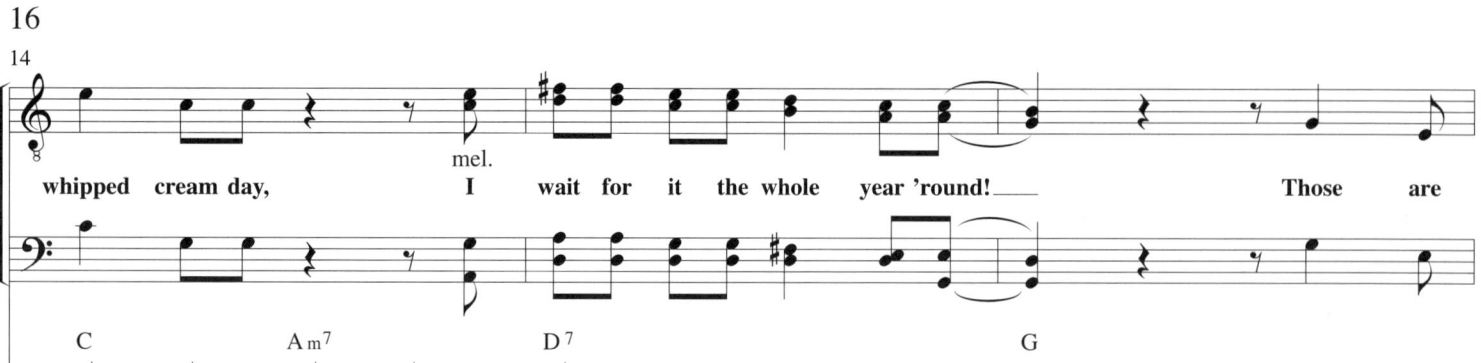

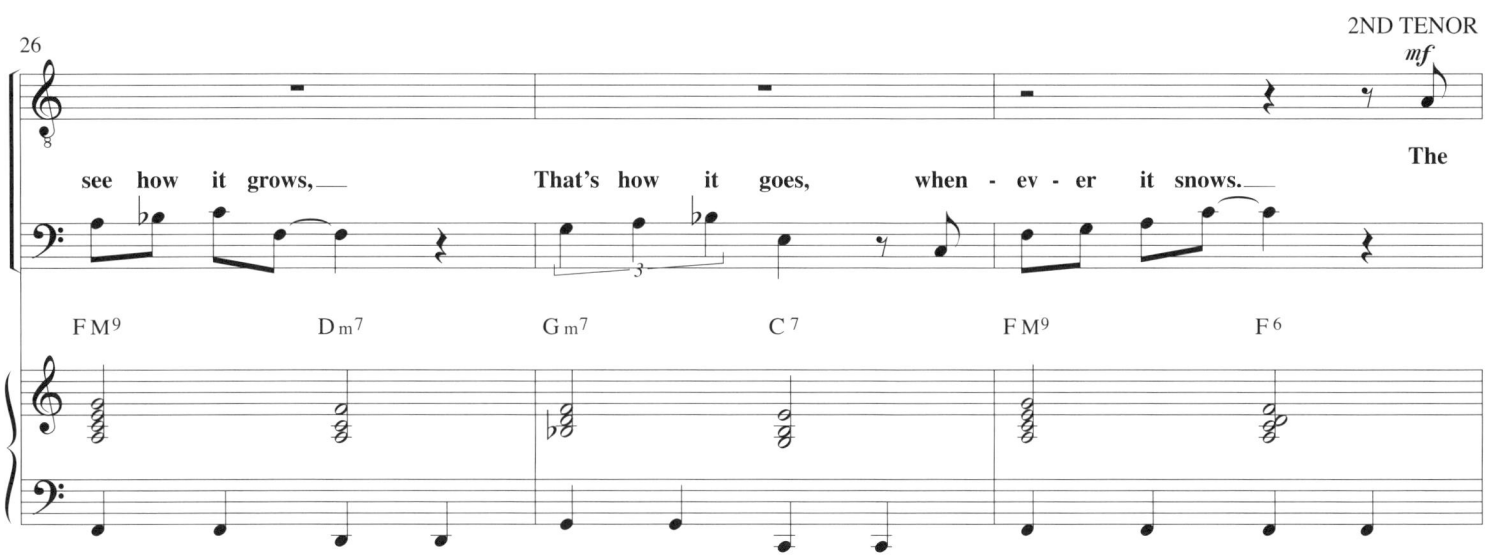

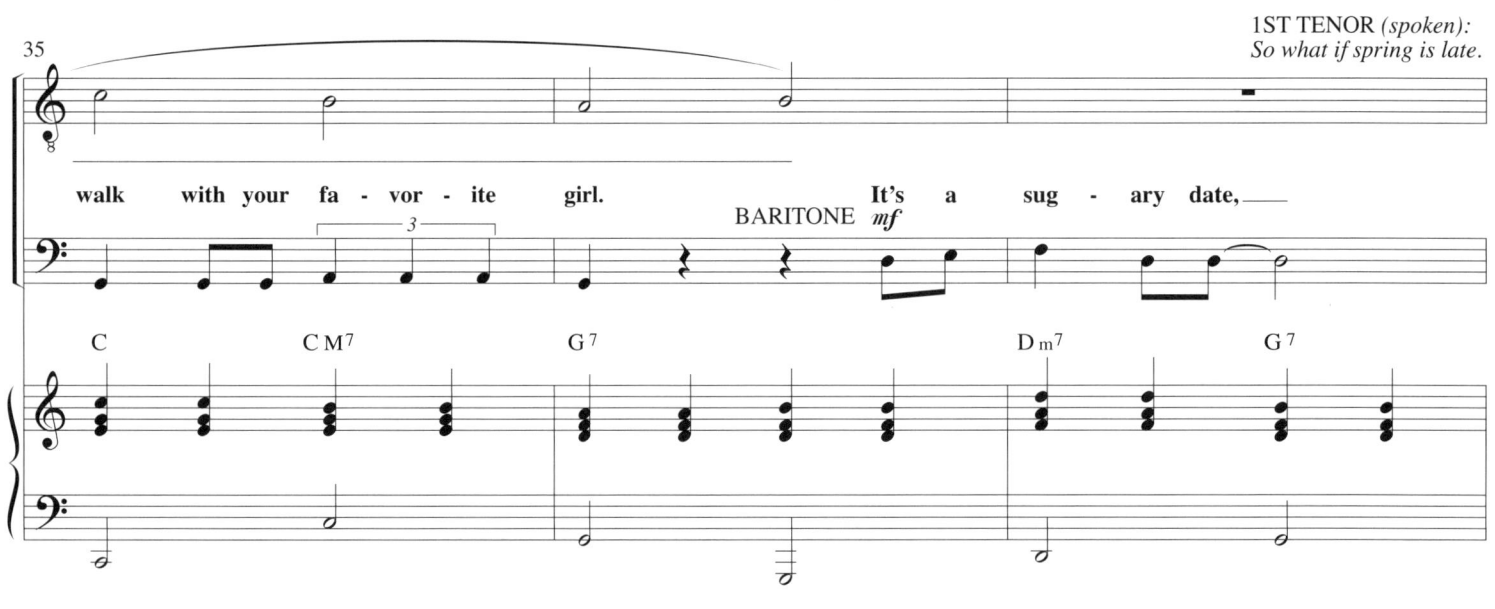
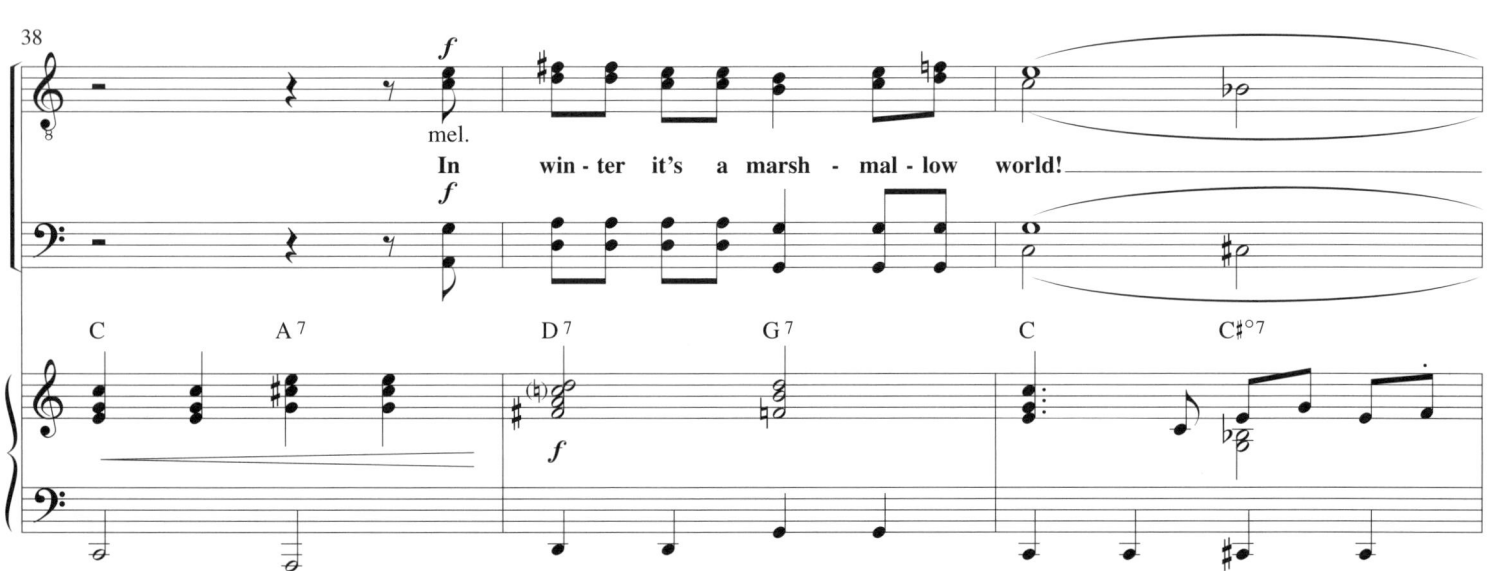

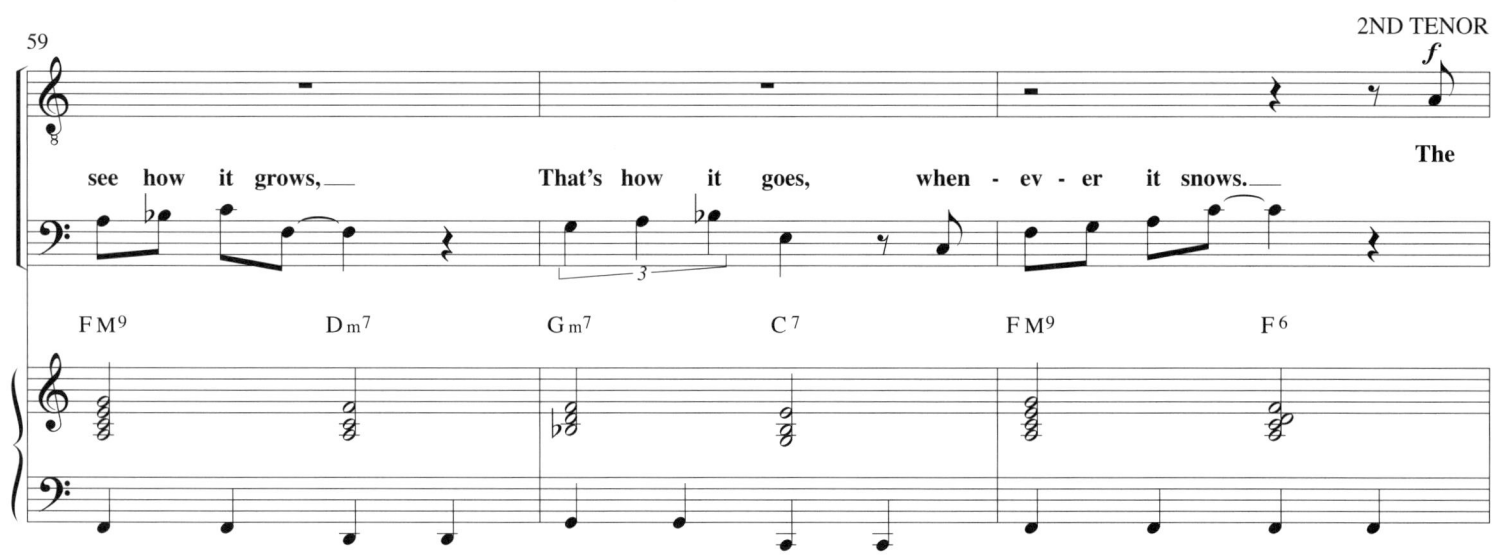
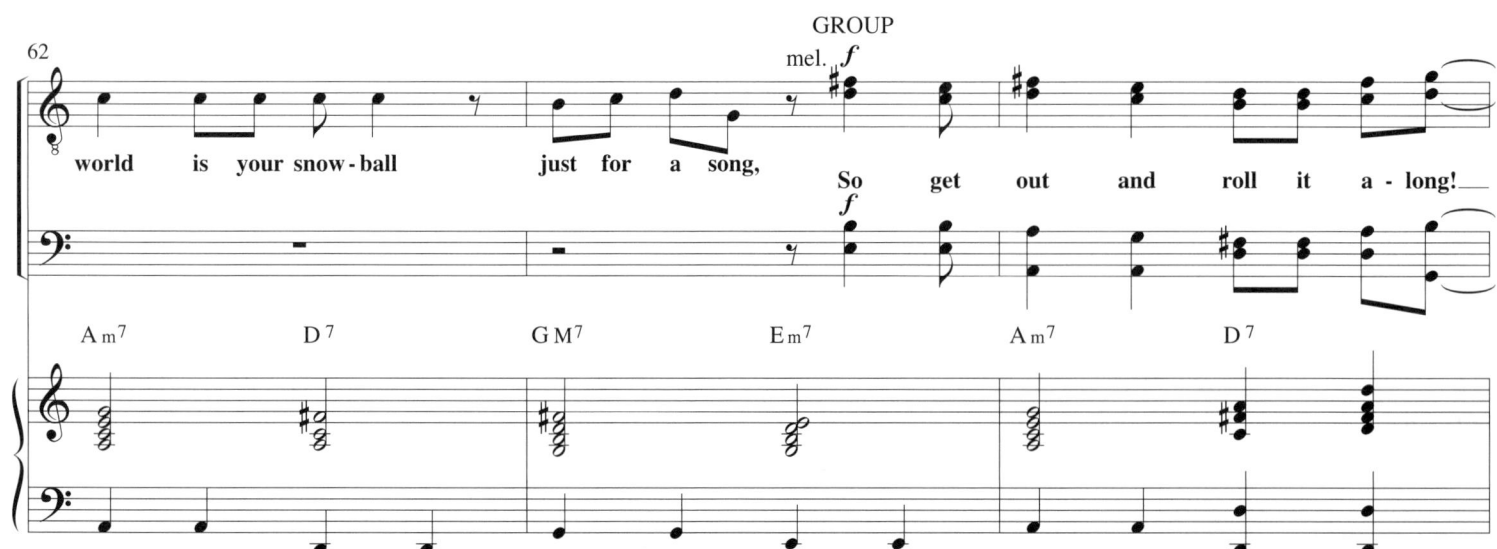

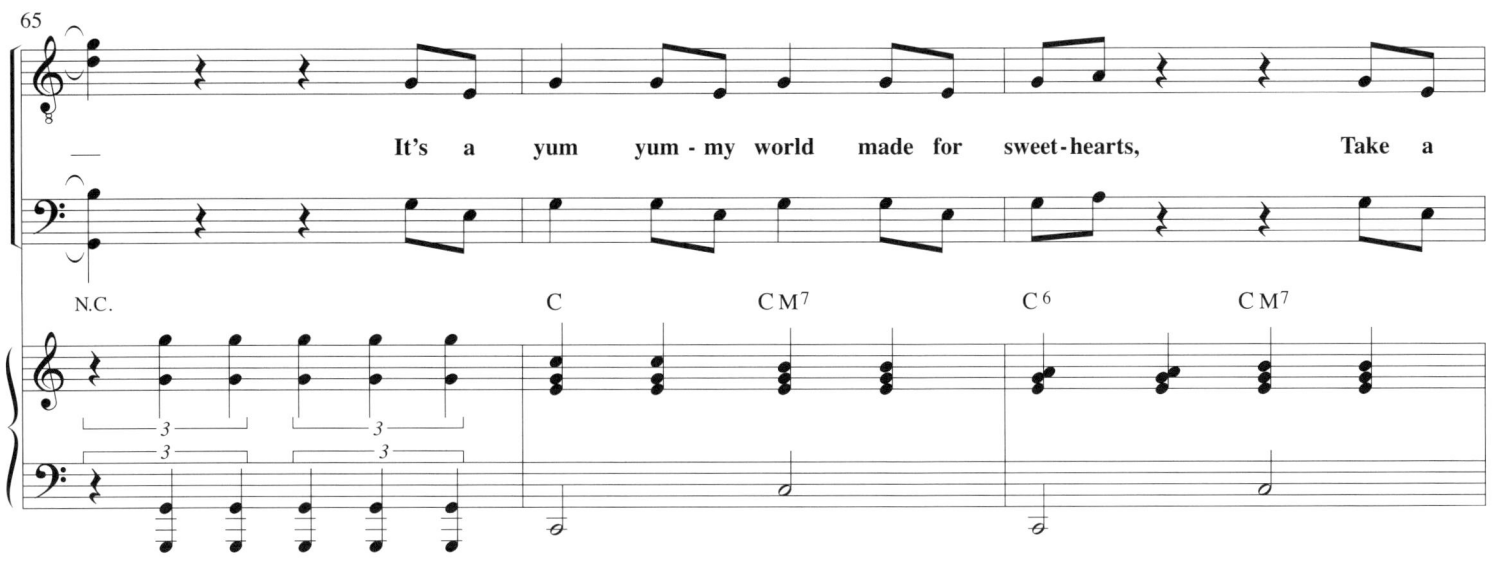
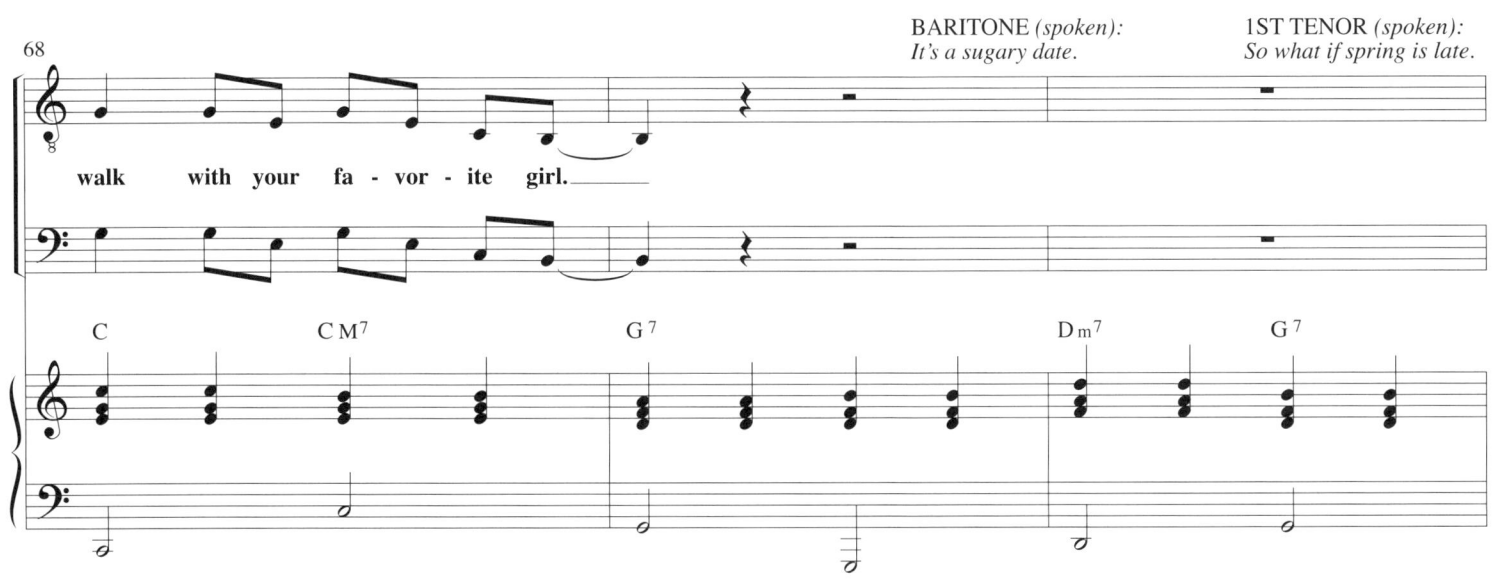

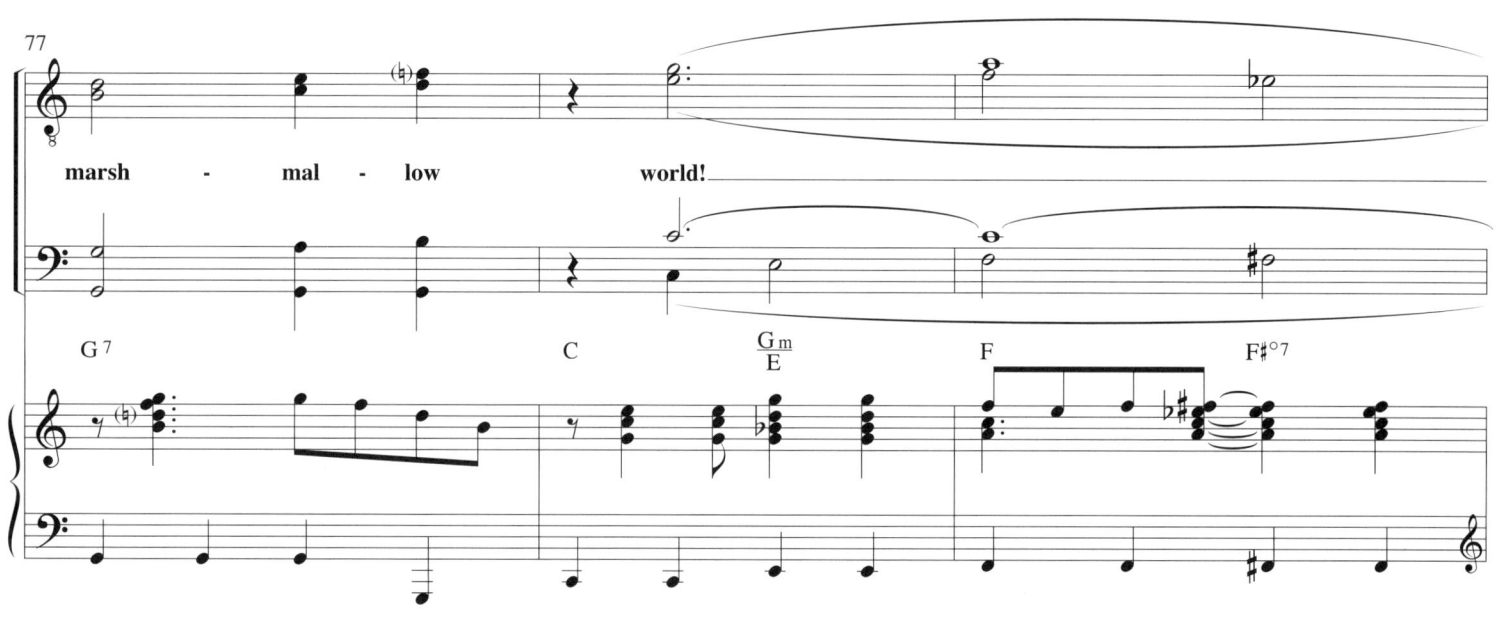

Every Light That Shines at Christmas

Words and Music by
ERNIE HAASE, WAYNE HAUN
and JOEL LINDSEY

© 2009 Ernie Sig Sound Music (BMI)/ PsalmSinger Music (BMI) (Administered by The Copyright Company)/
Universal Music-Brentwood-Benson Songs (BMI)/Universal-Brentwood-Benson Song/Hefton Hill Music (BMI). All rights reserved.

PLEASE NOTE: Copying of this product is NOT covered by CCLI licenses. For CCLI information call 1-800-234-2446.

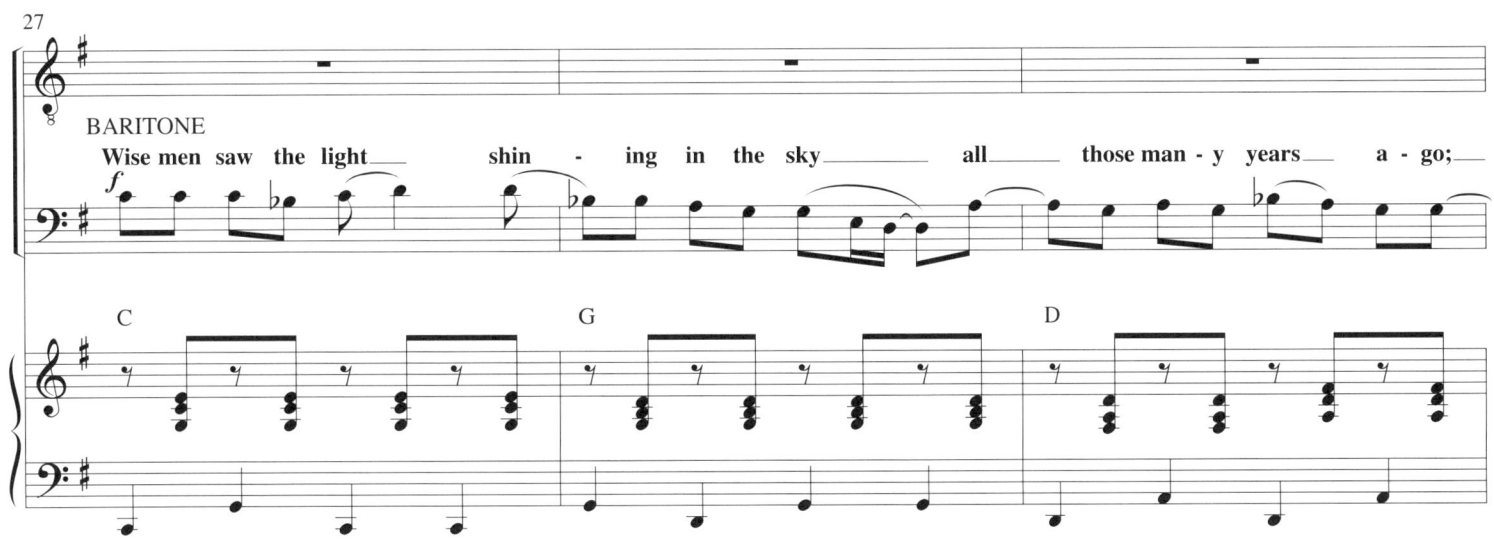
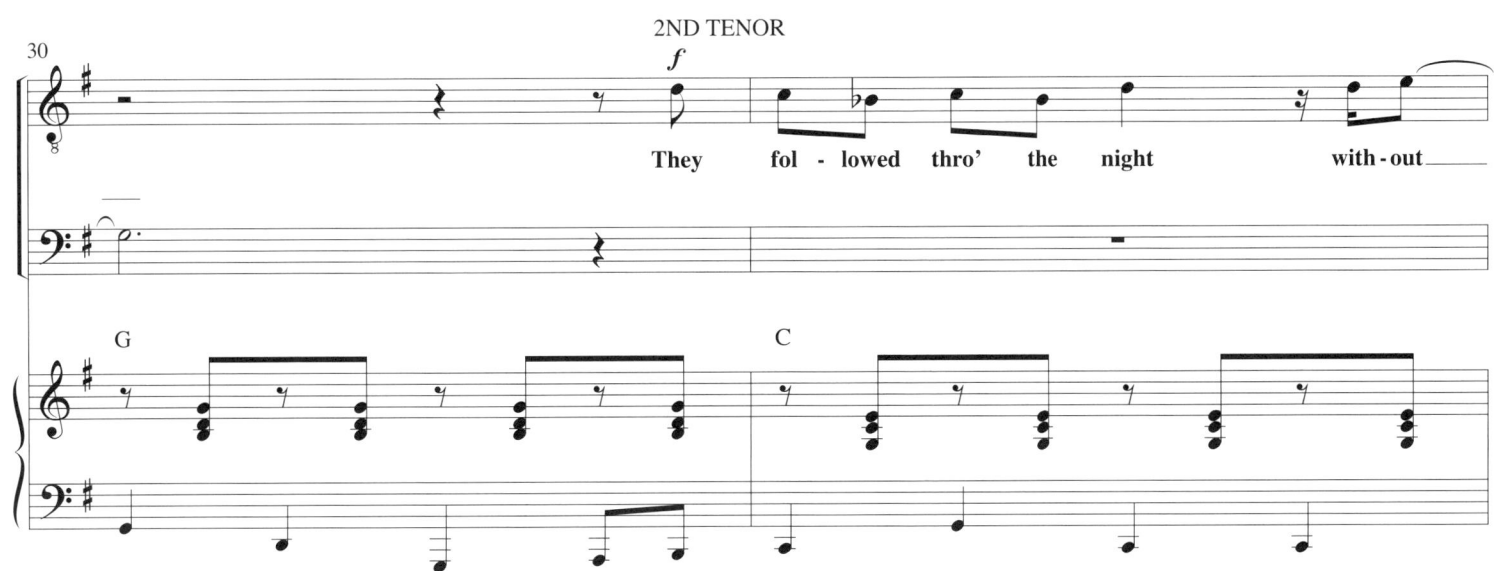

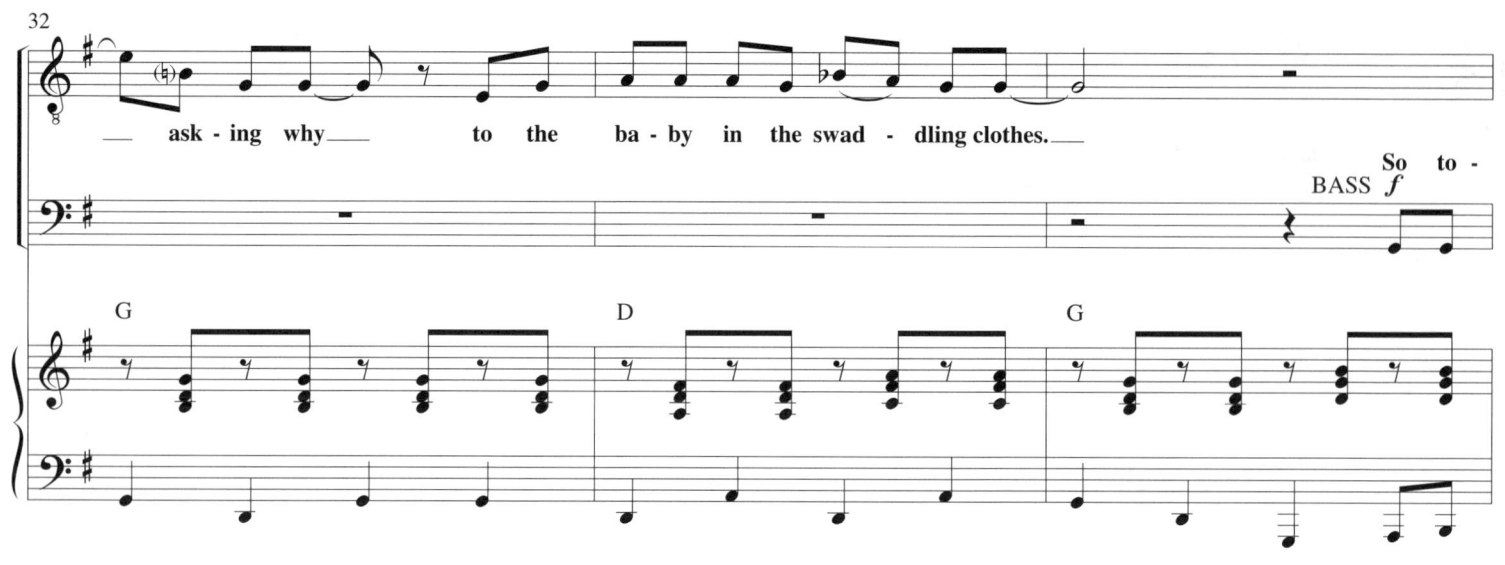

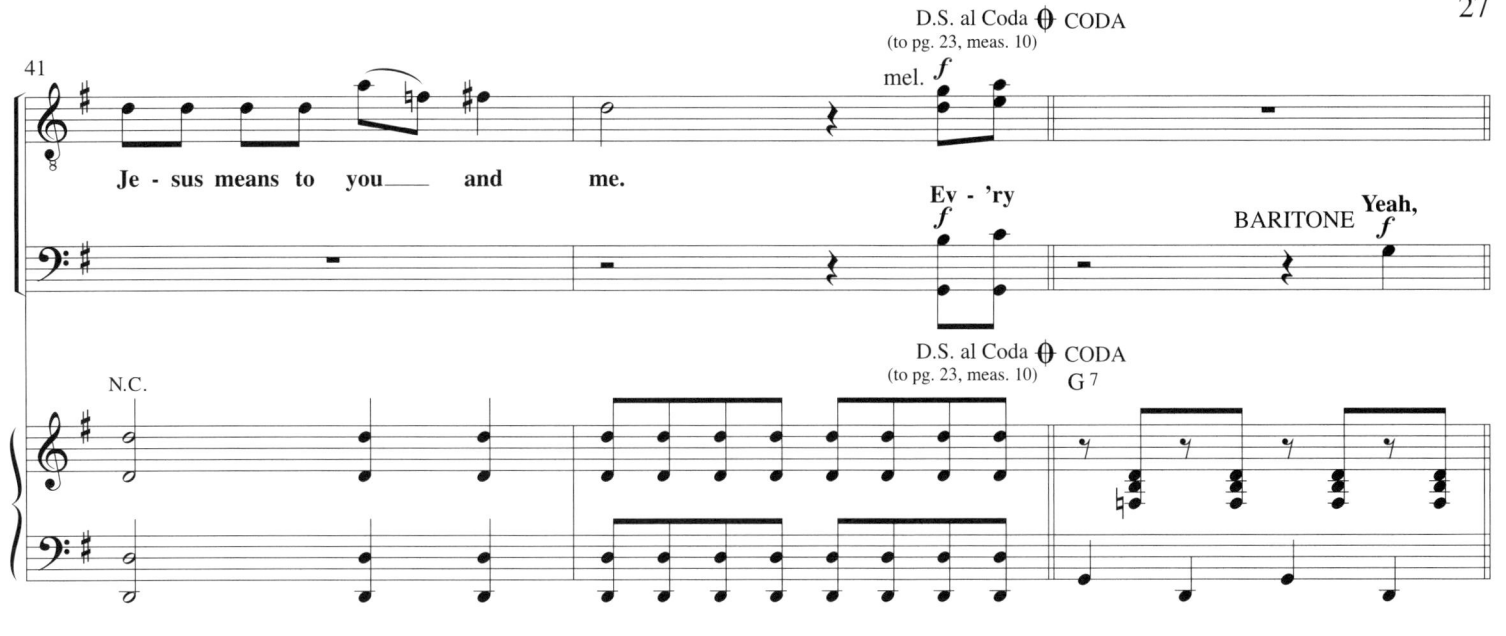

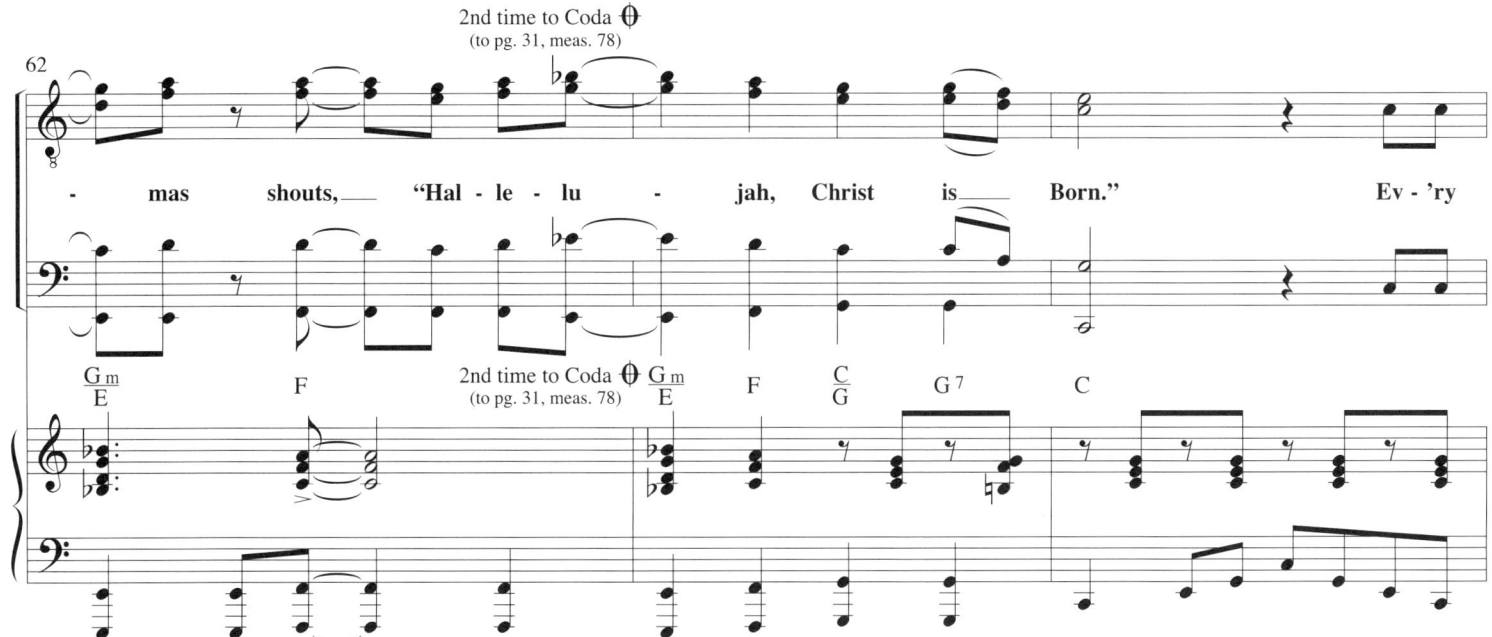

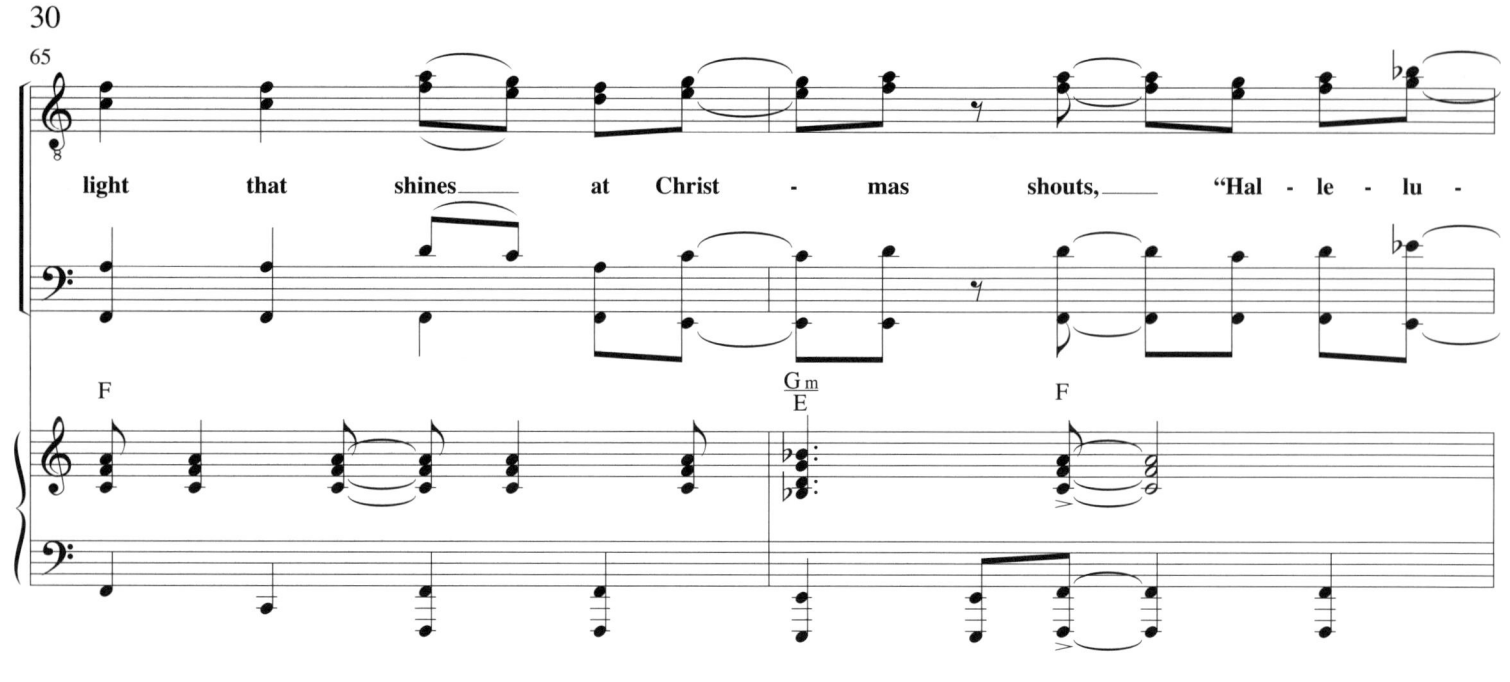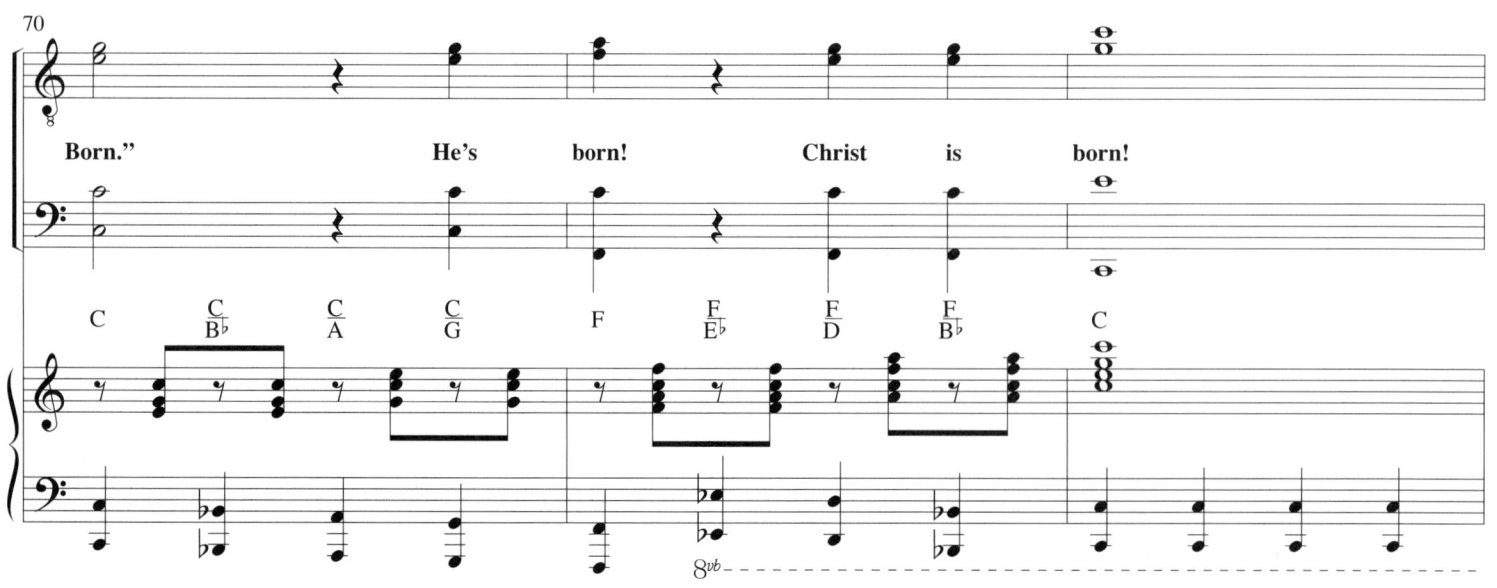

31

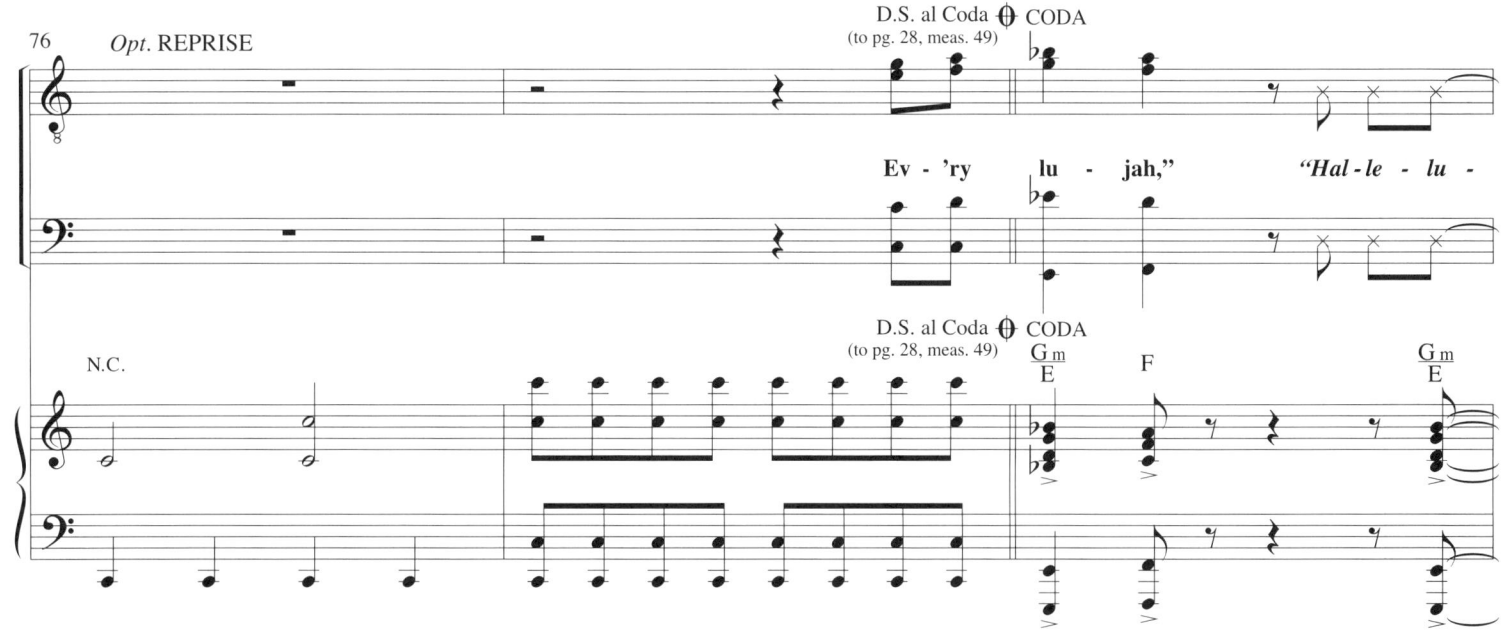

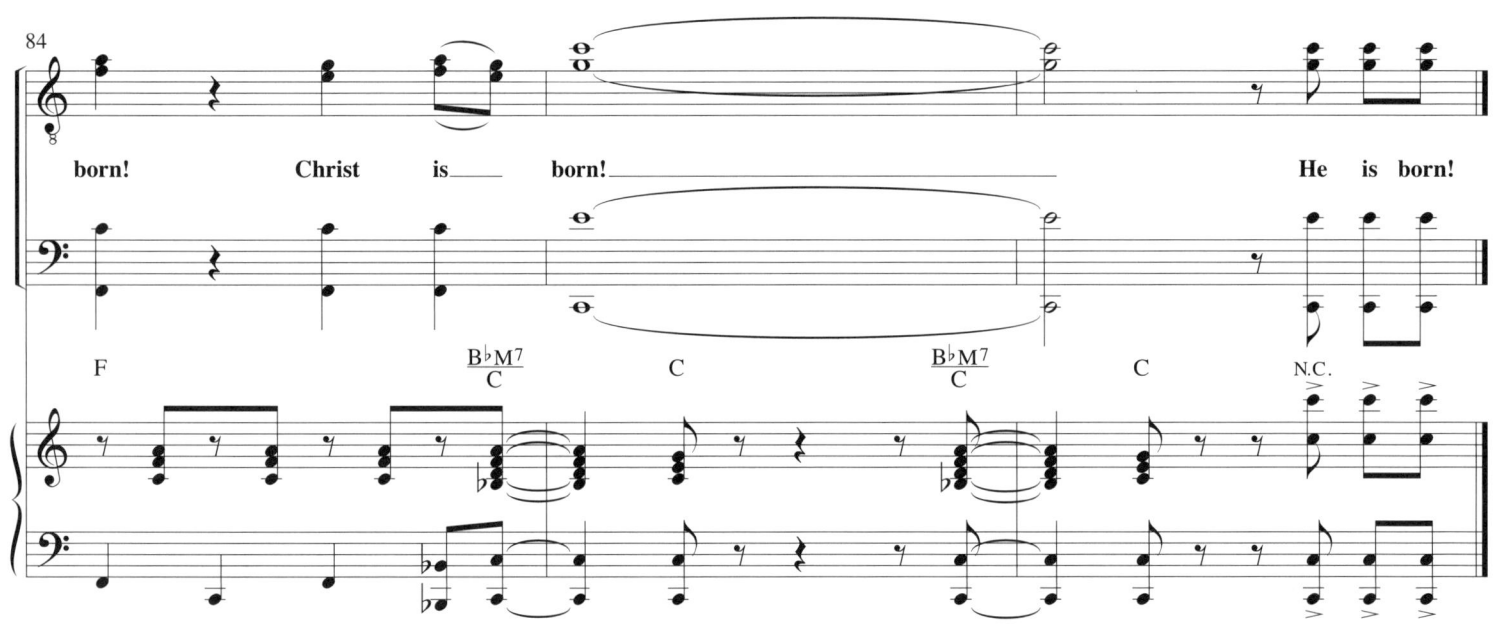

Redeeming Love

GLORIA GAITHER
BILL GAITHER

Copyright © 1971 William J. Gaither, Inc. /ASCAP. All rights controlled by Gaither Copyright Management. Used by permission.

PLEASE NOTE: Copying of this product is NOT covered by CCLI licenses. For CCLI information call 1-800-234-2446.

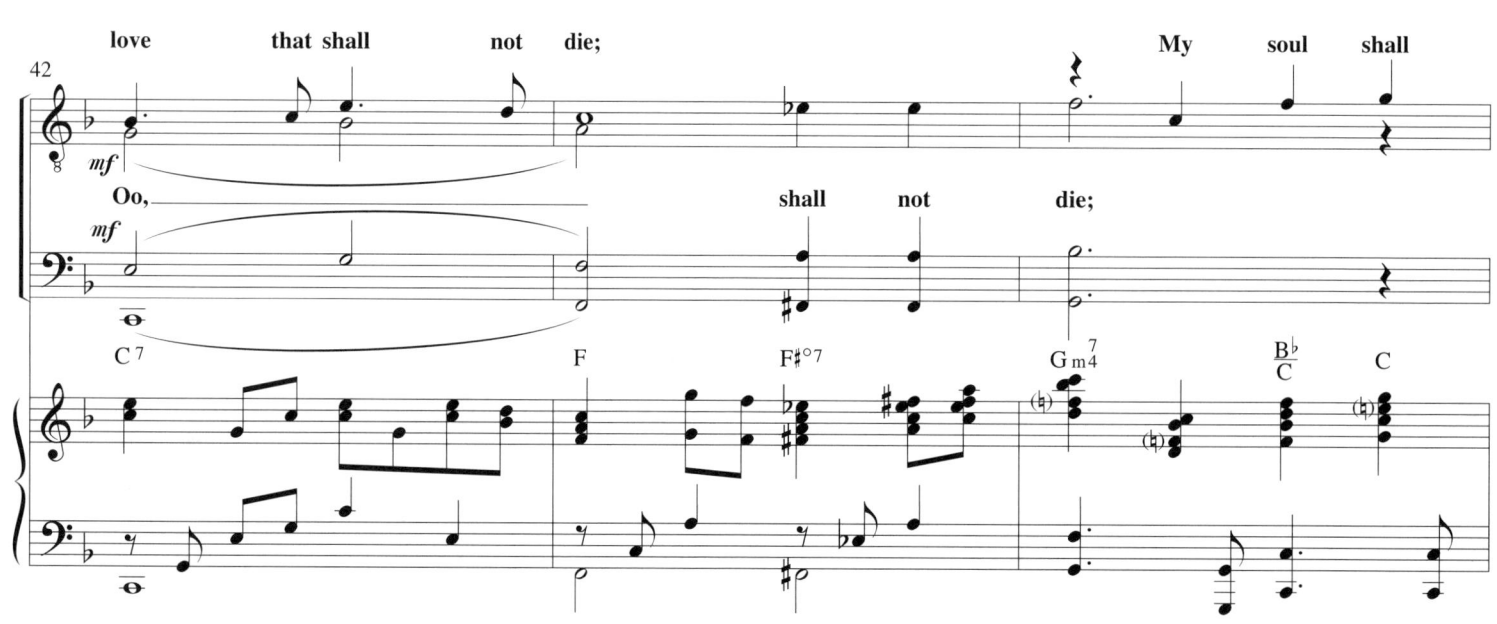

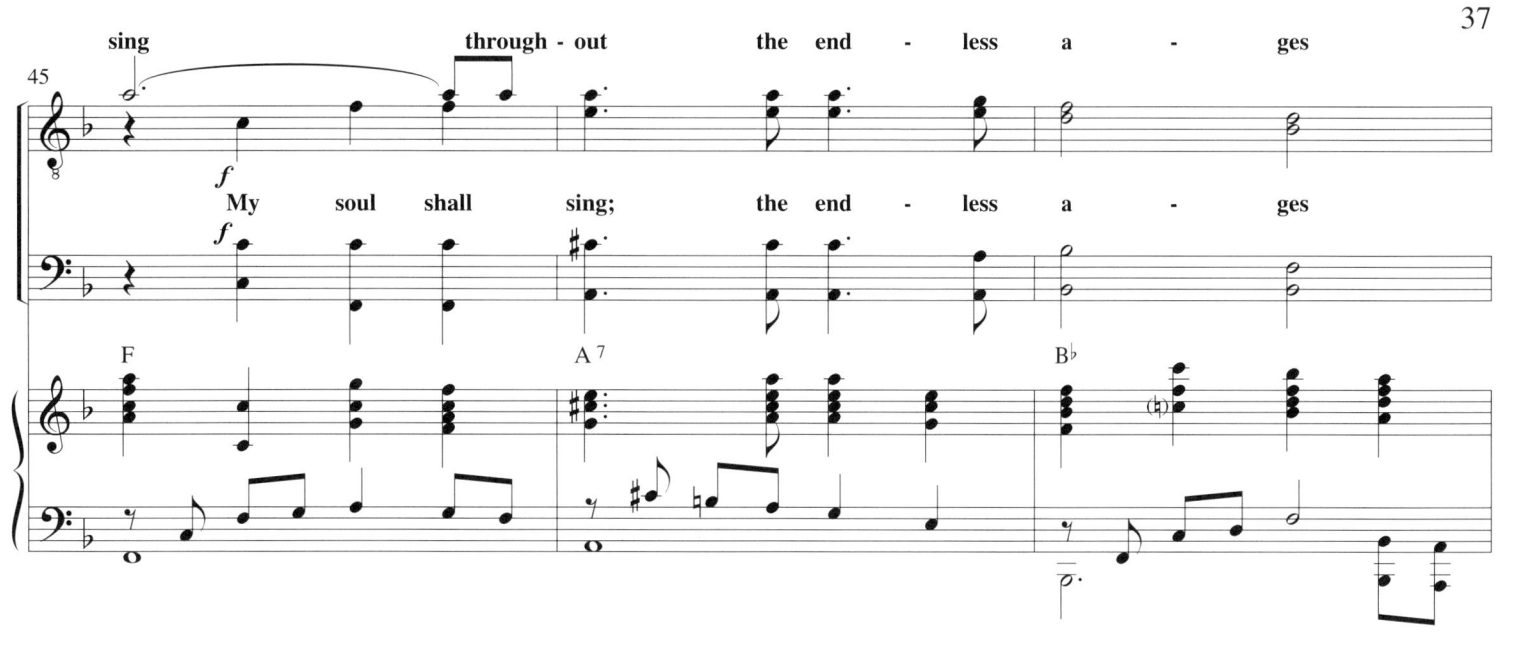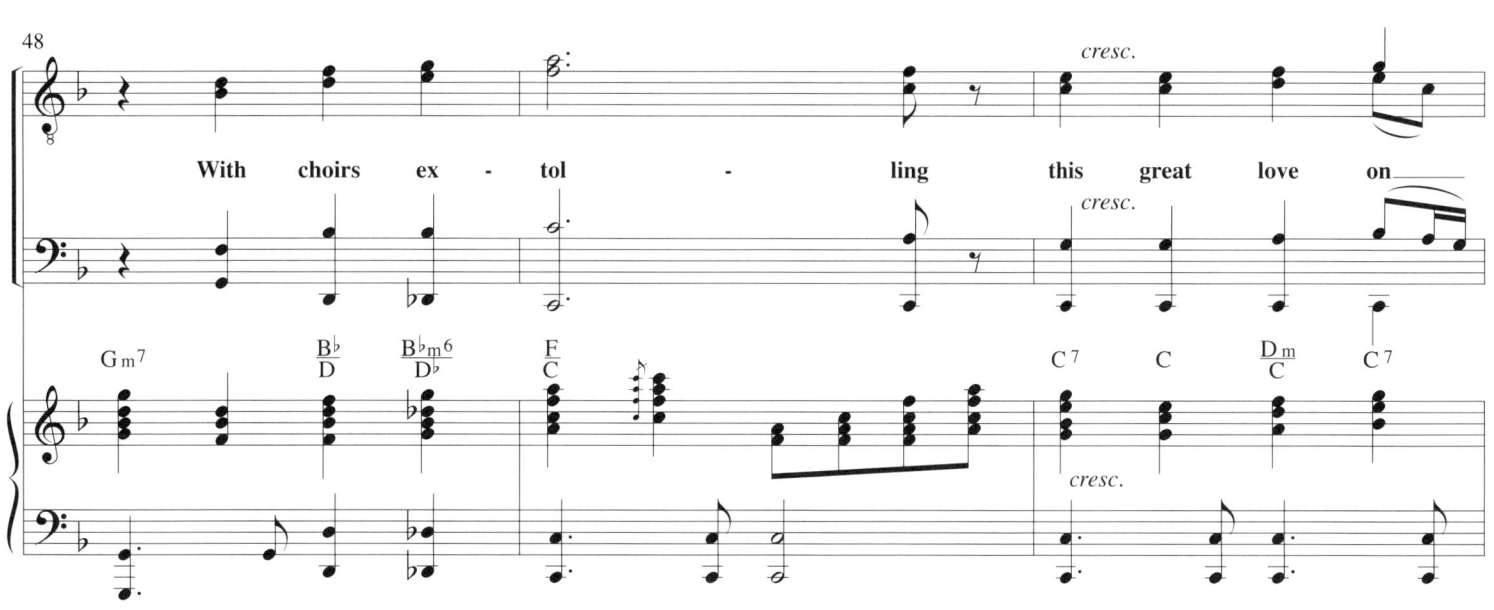

Changed by a Baby Boy

BENJAMIN GAITHER
and GLORIA GAITHER

BENJAMIN GAITHER

Copyright © 2006 Hook, Line and Music Publishing/Gaither Music Company/ASCAP.
All rights controlled by Gaither Copyright Management. Used by permission.

PLEASE NOTE: Copying of this product is NOT covered by CCLI licenses. For CCLI information call 1-800-234-2446.

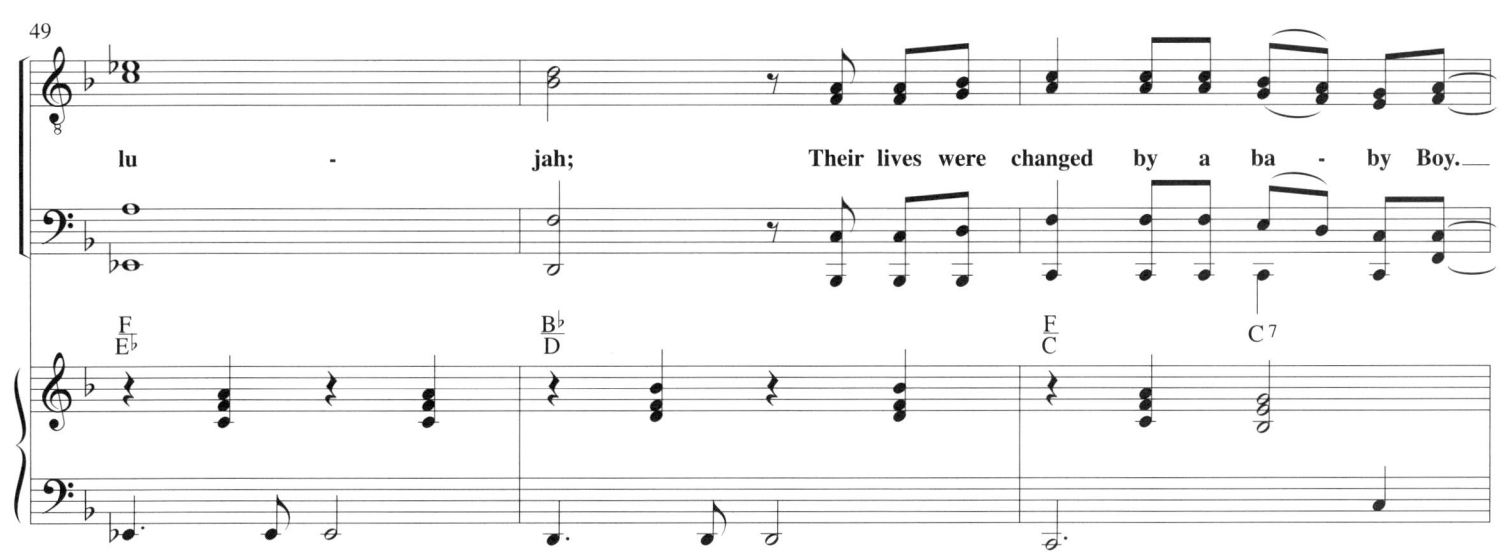

Mr. Heat Miser

Words and Music by
JULES BASS and
MAURY LAWS

1ST TENOR: *Whoa! Man, I hope Christmas this year is cold with lots of snow.*

BASS: *Not me. Because I like my Christmases warm and green.*

1ST TENOR: *Ah, that's because you're from the south.*

BASS: *And you're from the north.*

1ST TENOR: *That's right.*

(Lots of chatter)

BASS *(2nd time)*: *"Step aside, son, let me heat this thing up."*

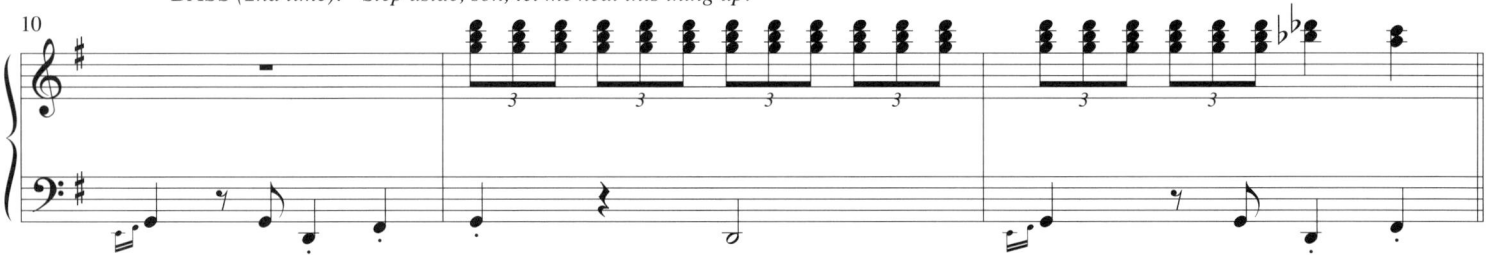

© 1974 (Renewed), 198 Lorimar Music A Corp. /ASCAP. All rights administered by Universal Music Corp.
Exclusive print rights administered by Alfred Music Publishing Co., Inc. All rights reserved. Used by permission.

PLEASE NOTE: Copying of this product is NOT covered by CCLI licenses. For CCLI information call 1-800-234-2446.

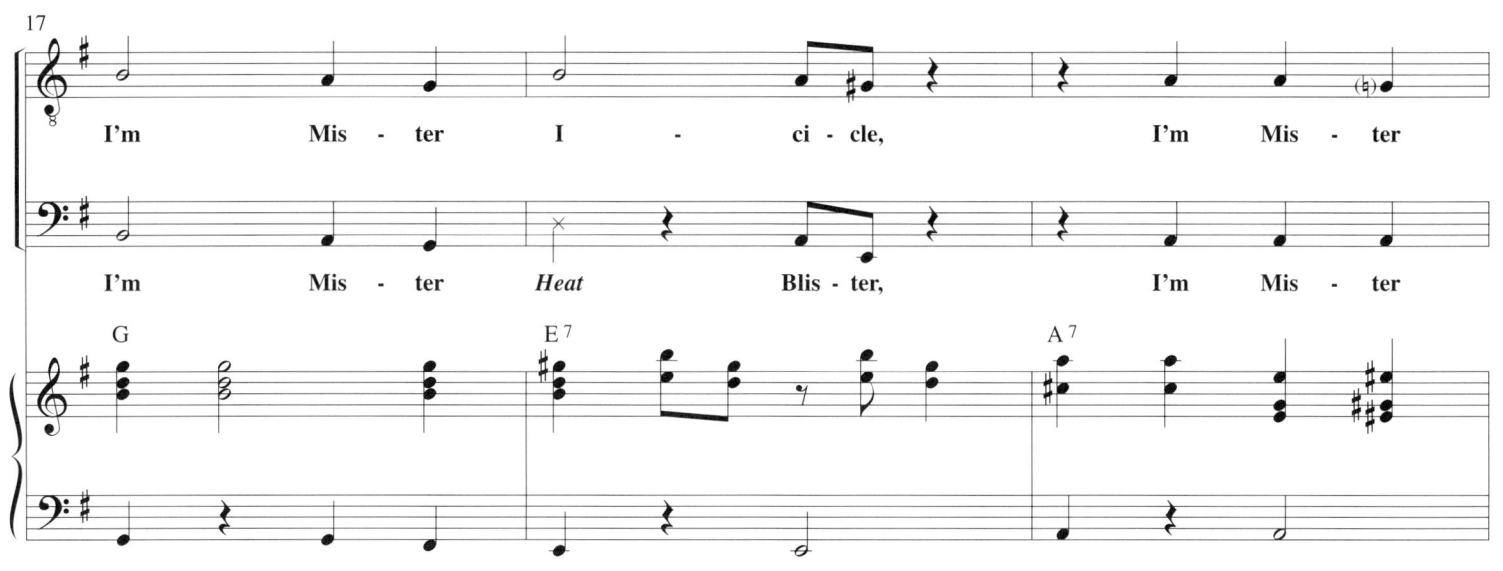

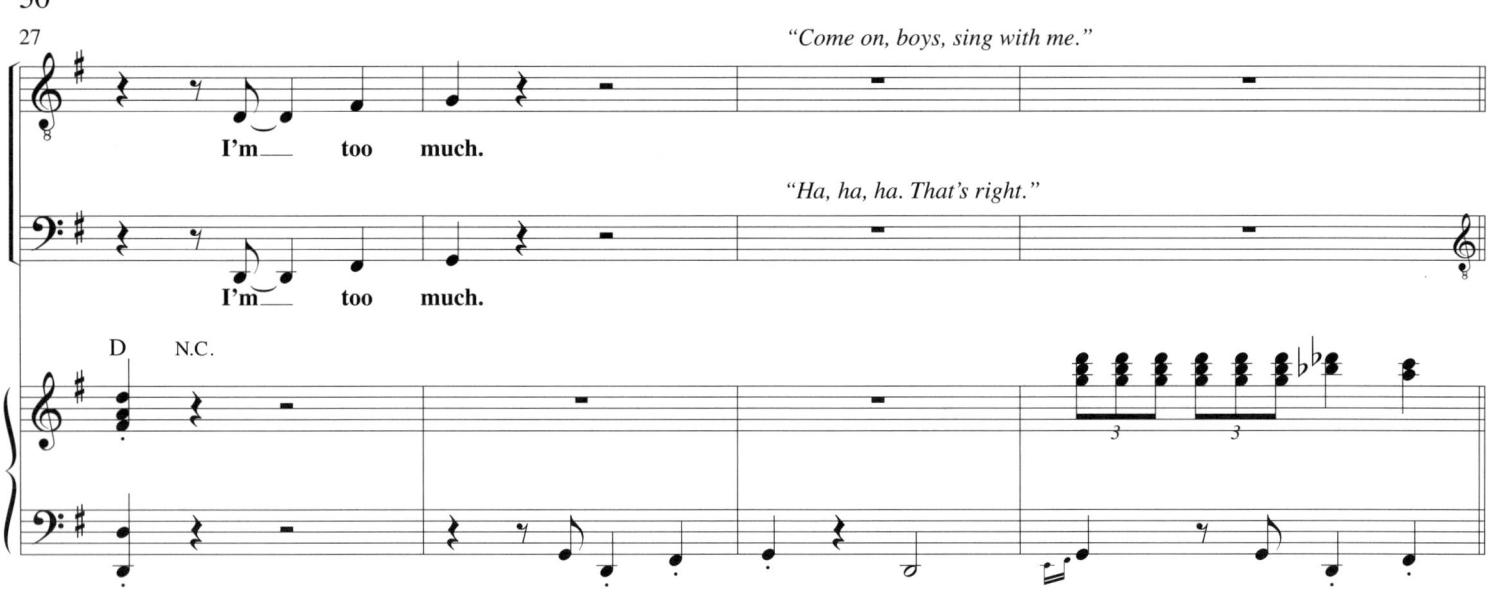

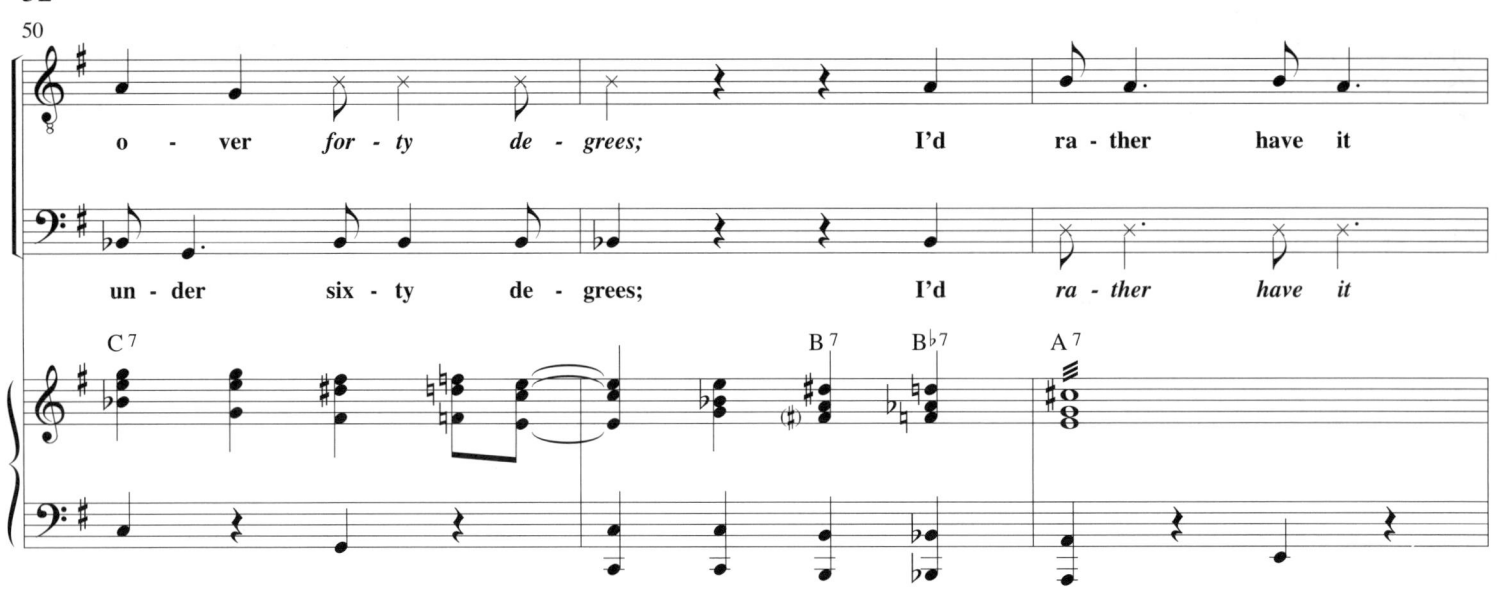

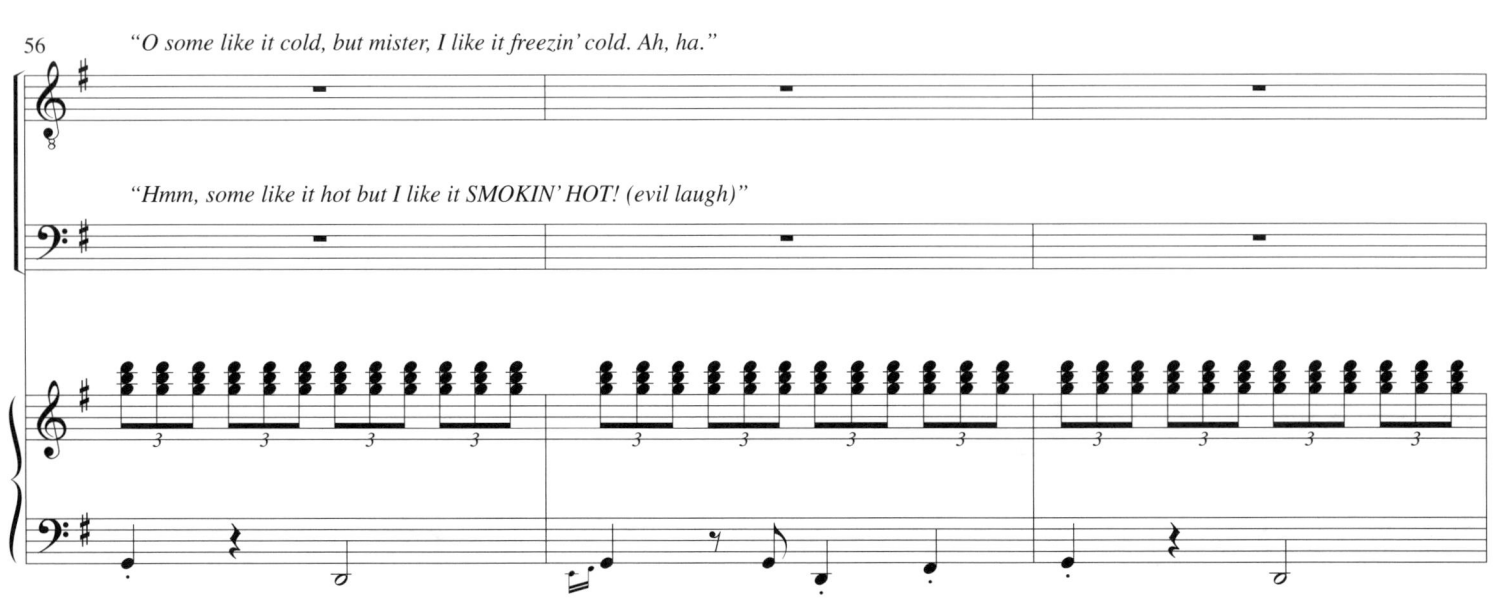

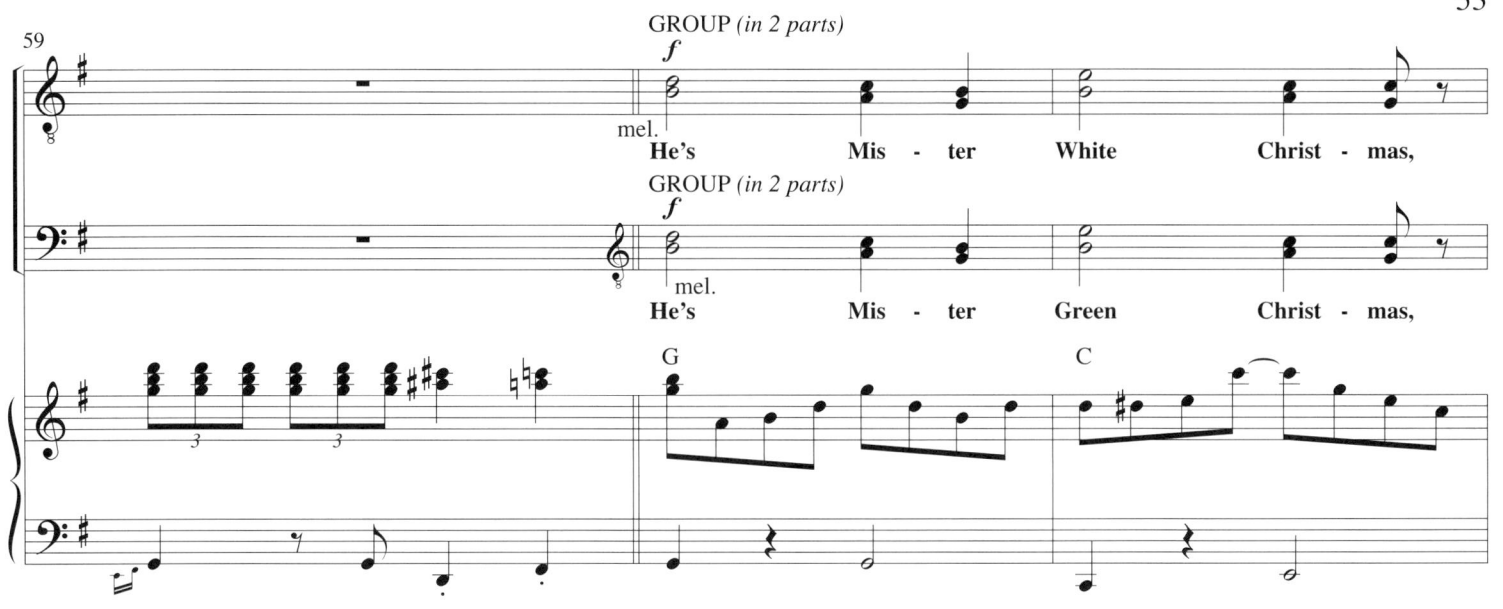

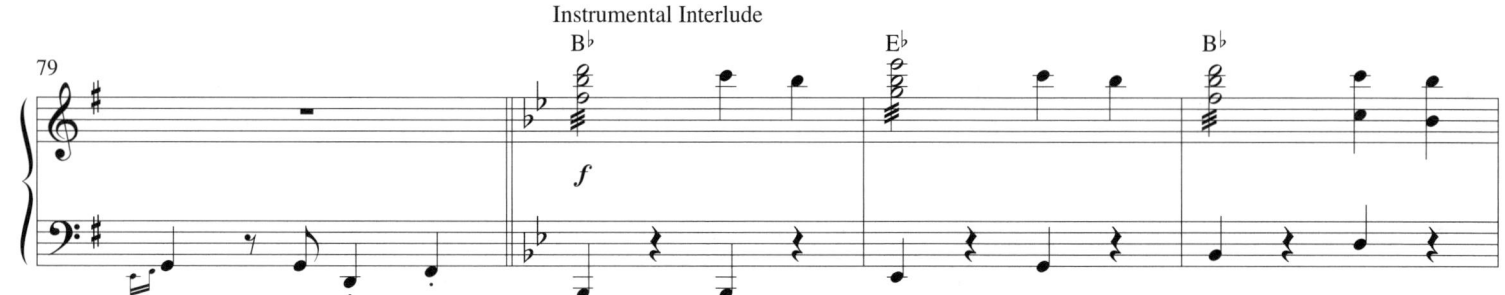

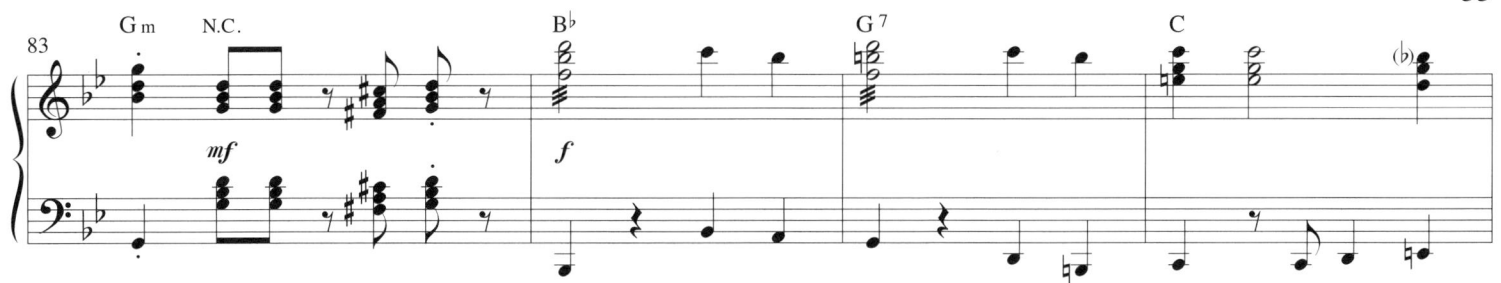
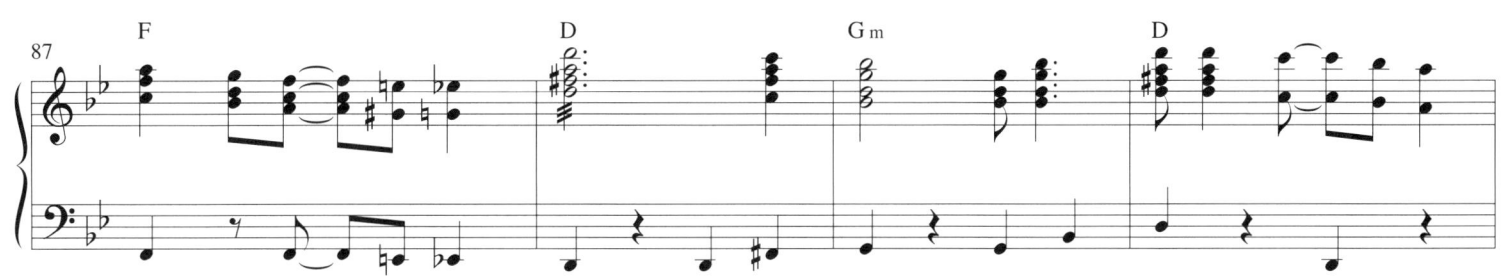

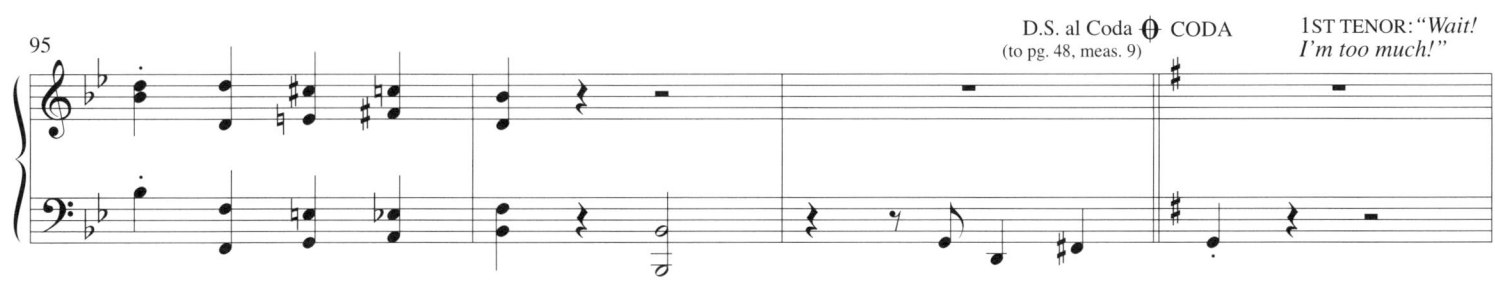

Thank God for Kids

Words and Music by
EDDY RAVEN

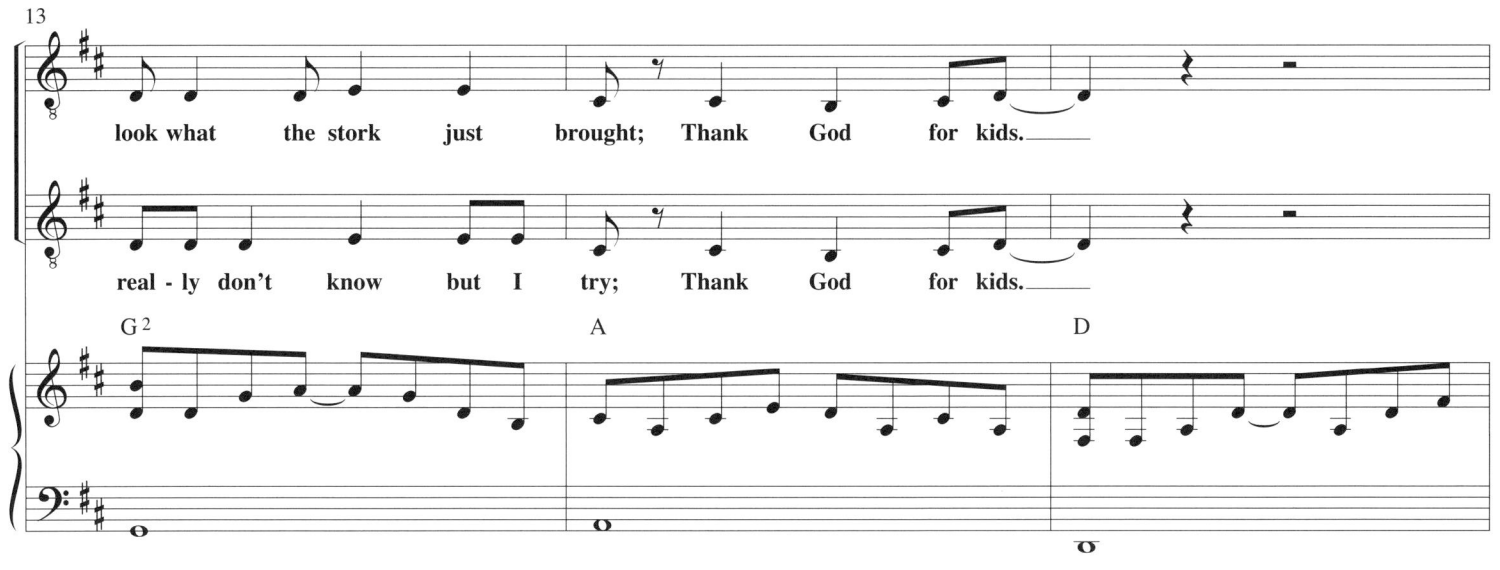

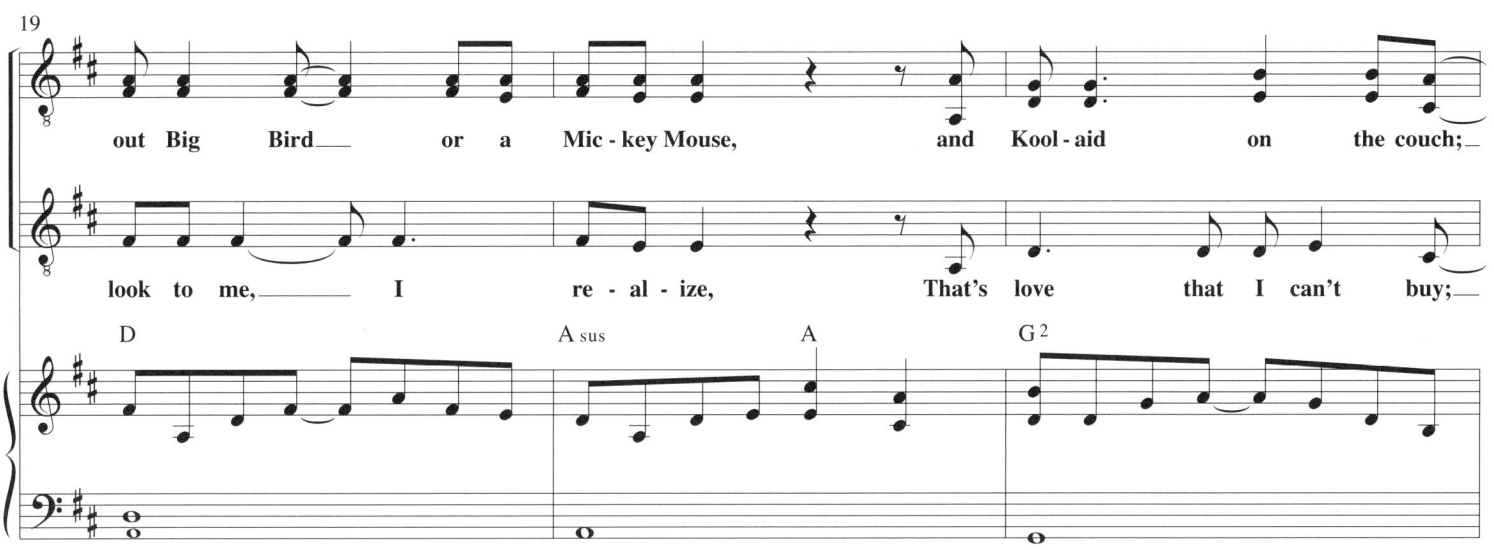

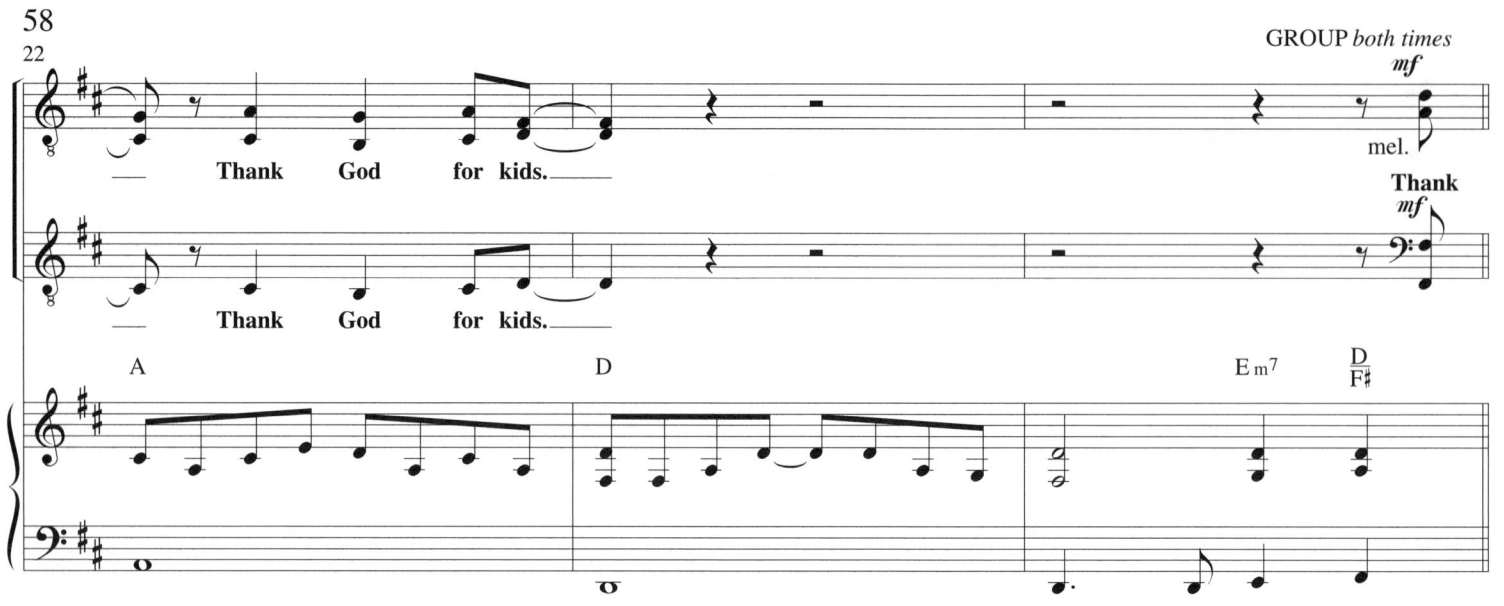

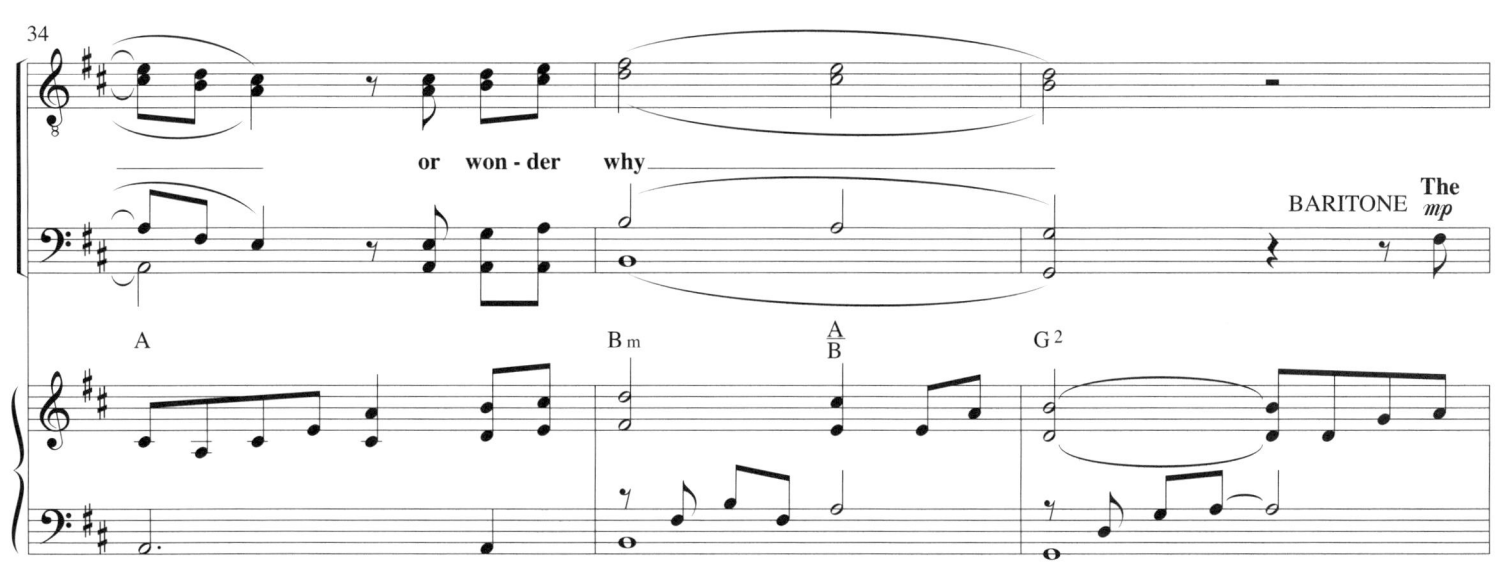
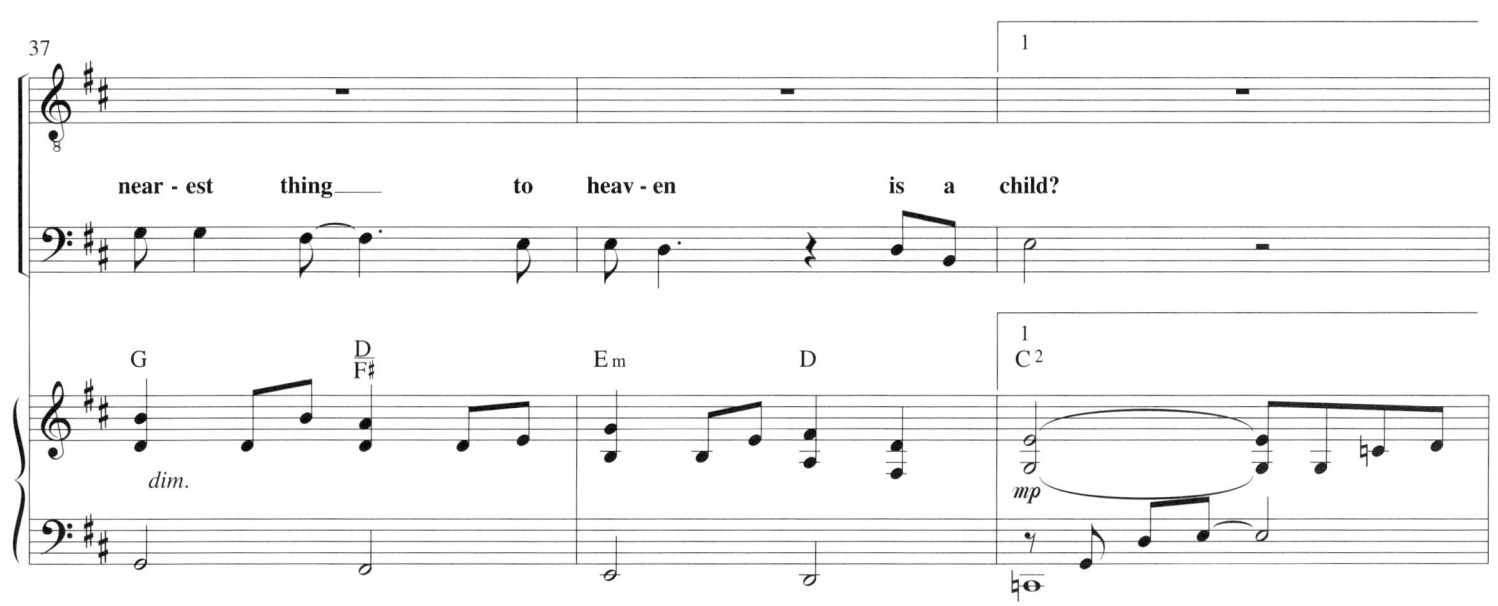

Christmas Is Christmas
(Wherever You Are)

Words and Music by
WAYNE HAUN, SHELBY HAUN
and JOEL LINDSEY

© 2008 PsalmSinger Music (BMI) (Administered by The Copyright Company)/
Bridge Building (BMI)/ Hefton Hill Music (BMI). All rights reserved.

PLEASE NOTE: Copying of this product is NOT covered by CCLI licenses. For CCLI information call 1-800-234-2446.

God Rest Ye Merry, Gentlemen
A cappella

English Carol   English Melody

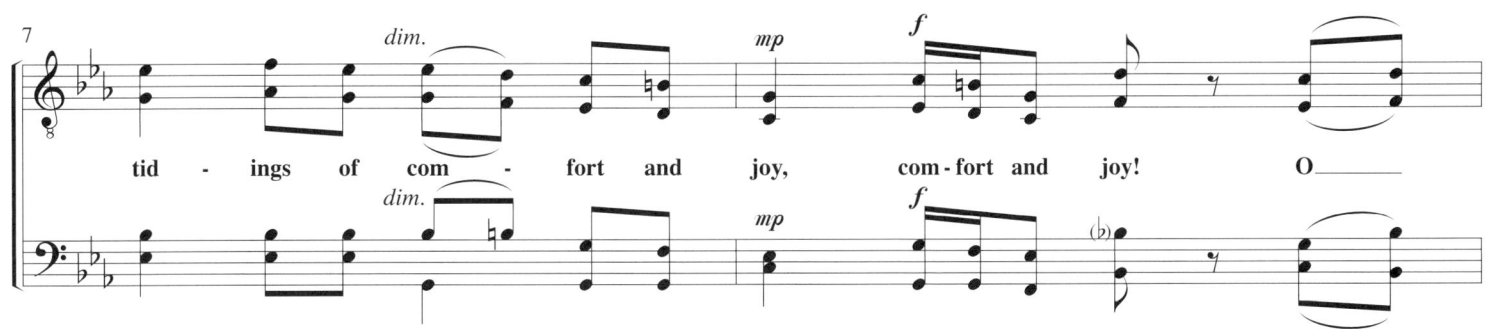

Arr. © 2009 PsalmSinger Music (BMI) (Administered by The Copyright Company)/Ernie Sig Sound Music (BMI). All rights reserved.

PLEASE NOTE: Copying of this product is NOT covered by CCLI licenses. For CCLI information call 1-800-234-2446.

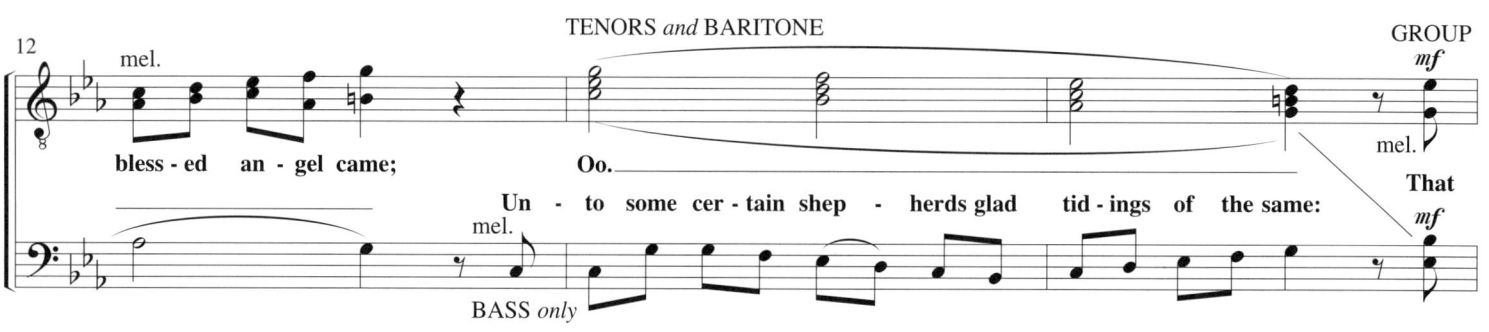

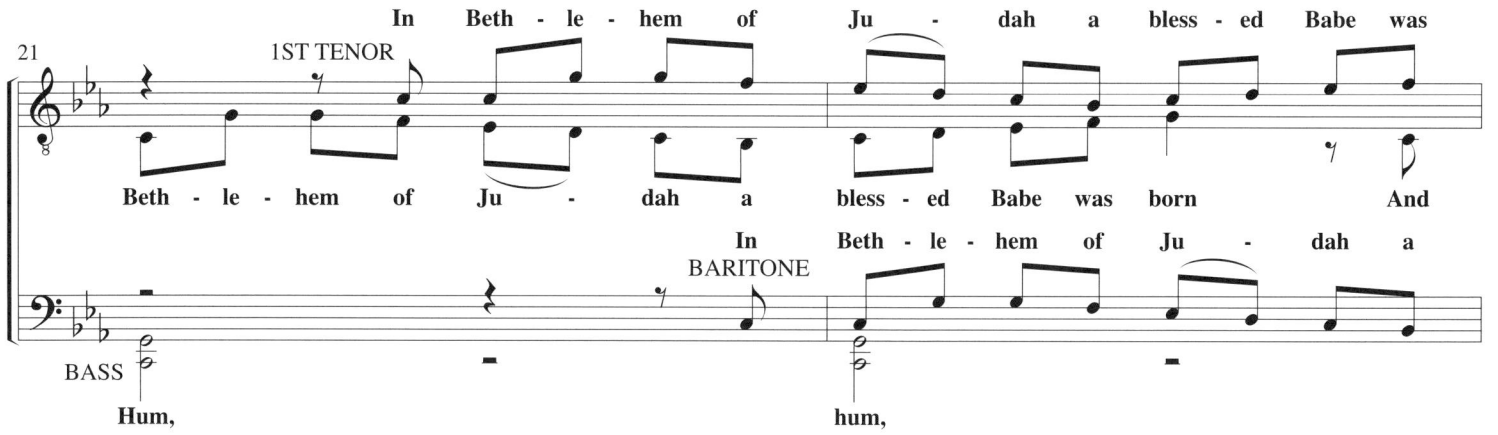

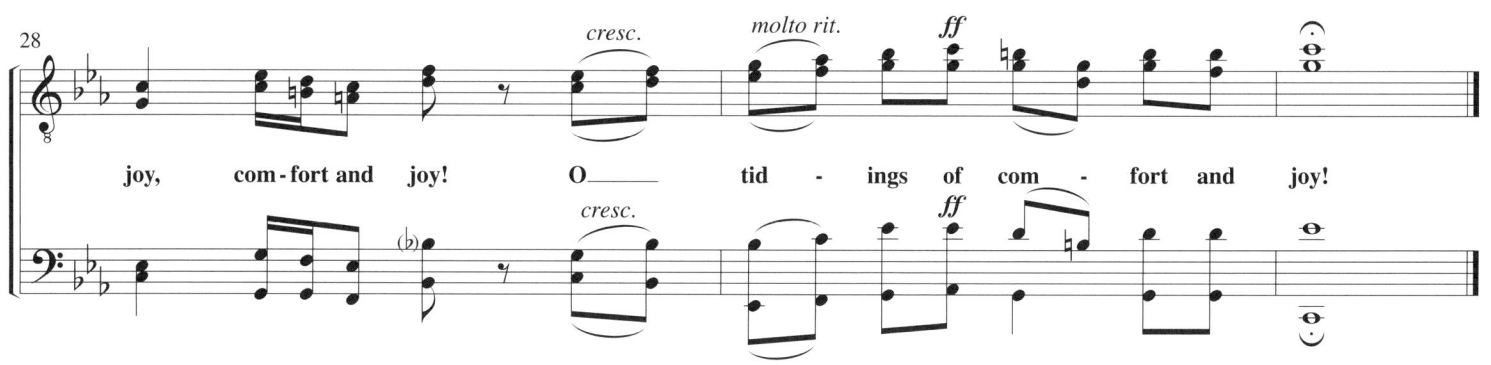

If It Doesn't Snow on Christmas

Words and Music by
MILTON PASCAL and
GERALD MARKS

Santa works all day in his work-shop Making lots of games and toys;

Then one day, he hops in his sleigh And brings them to the girls and boys;

© 1949 (Copyright Renewed) and this arr. © 2009 Lombardo Music, Inc. (ASCAP)/ Gerald Marks Music (ASCAP).
All rights for Lombardo Music, Inc. administered by WB Music Corp. All rights for Gerald Marks Music, Inc.
administered by Sony/ATV Music Publishing, LLC, 8 Music Square West, Nashville, TN 37203.
International copyrights secured. All rights reserved. Used by permission.

PLEASE NOTE: Copying of this product is NOT covered by CCLI licenses. For CCLI information call 1-800-234-2446.

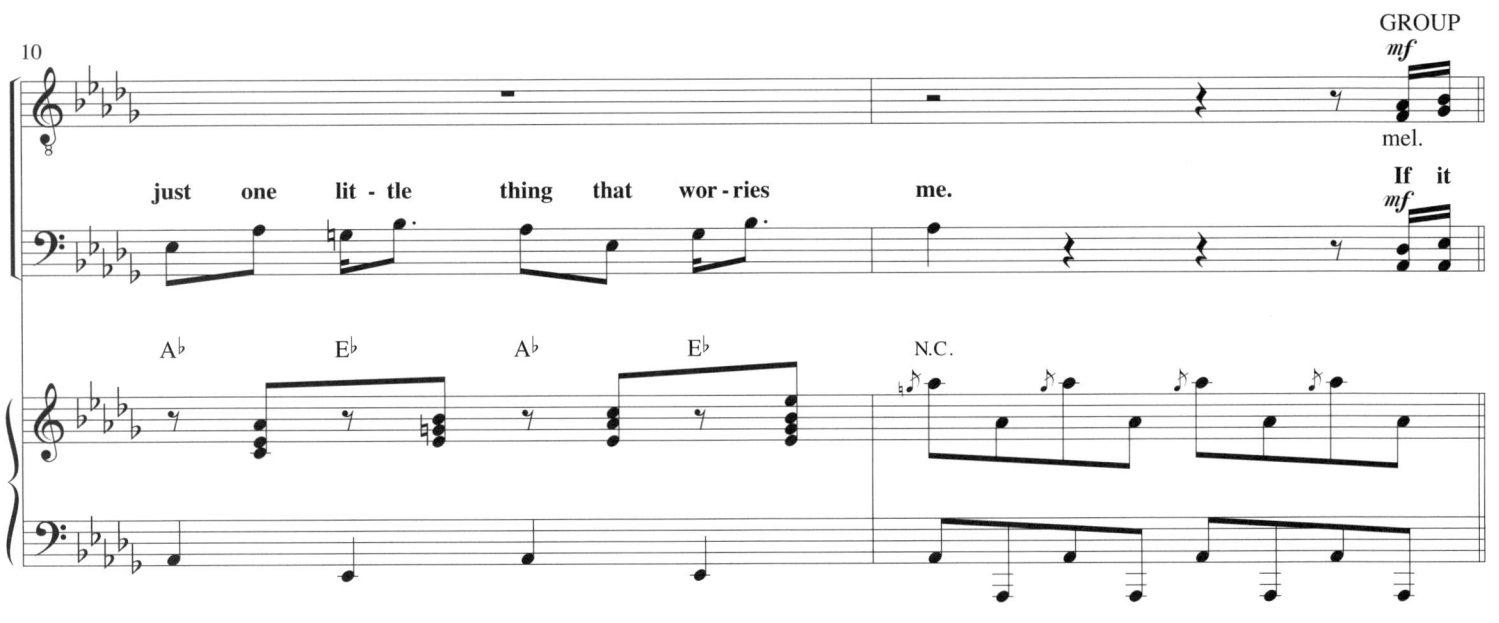

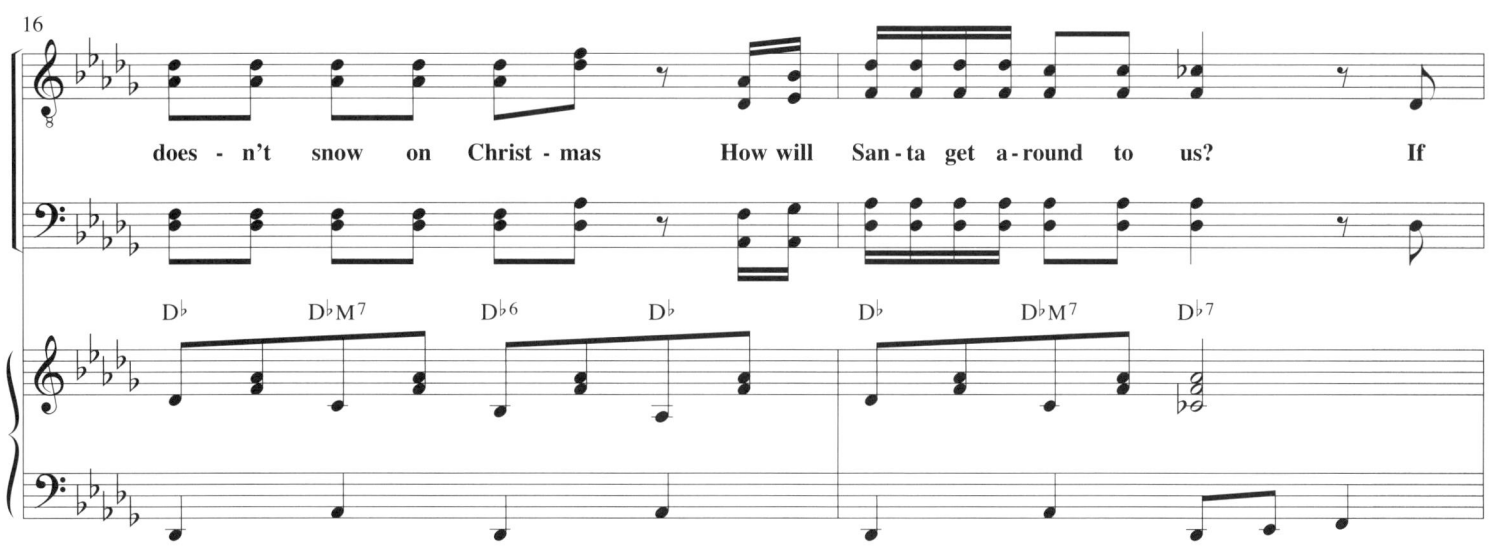
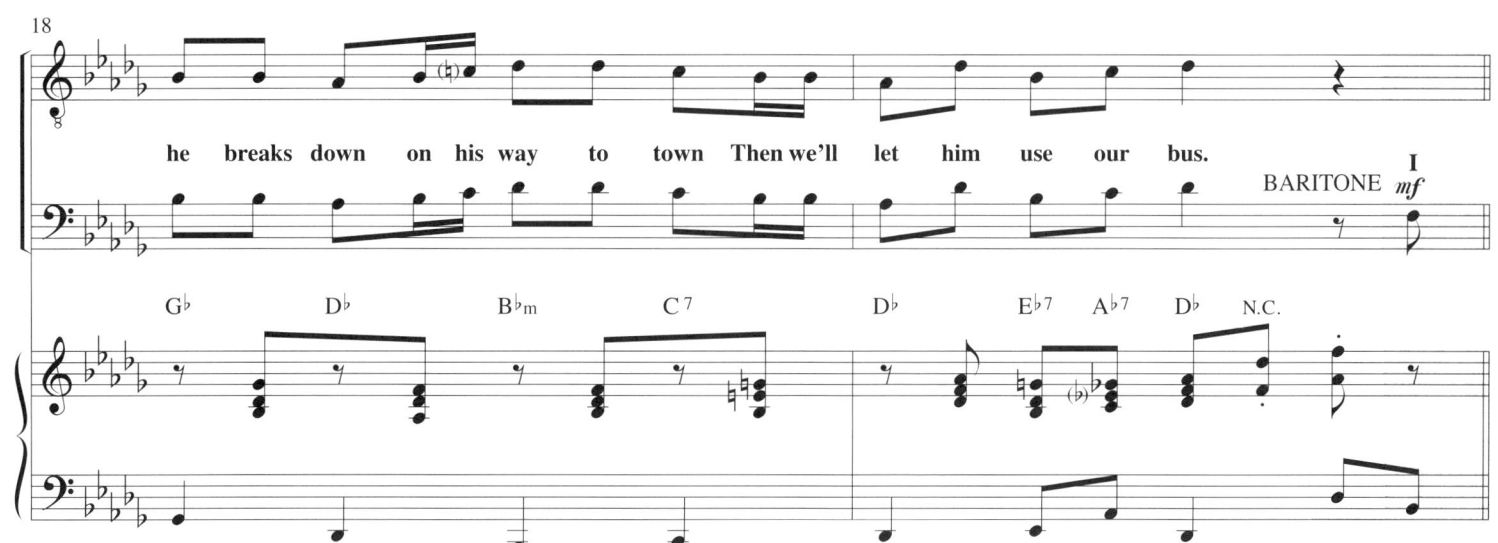

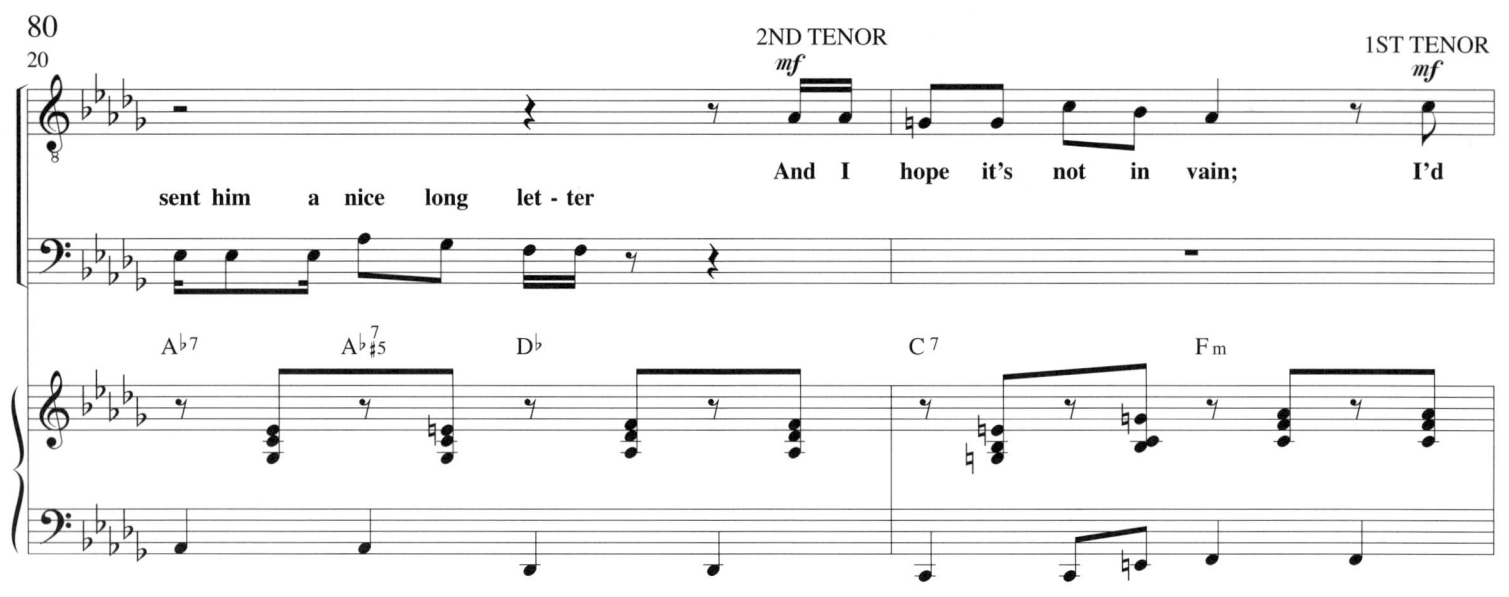
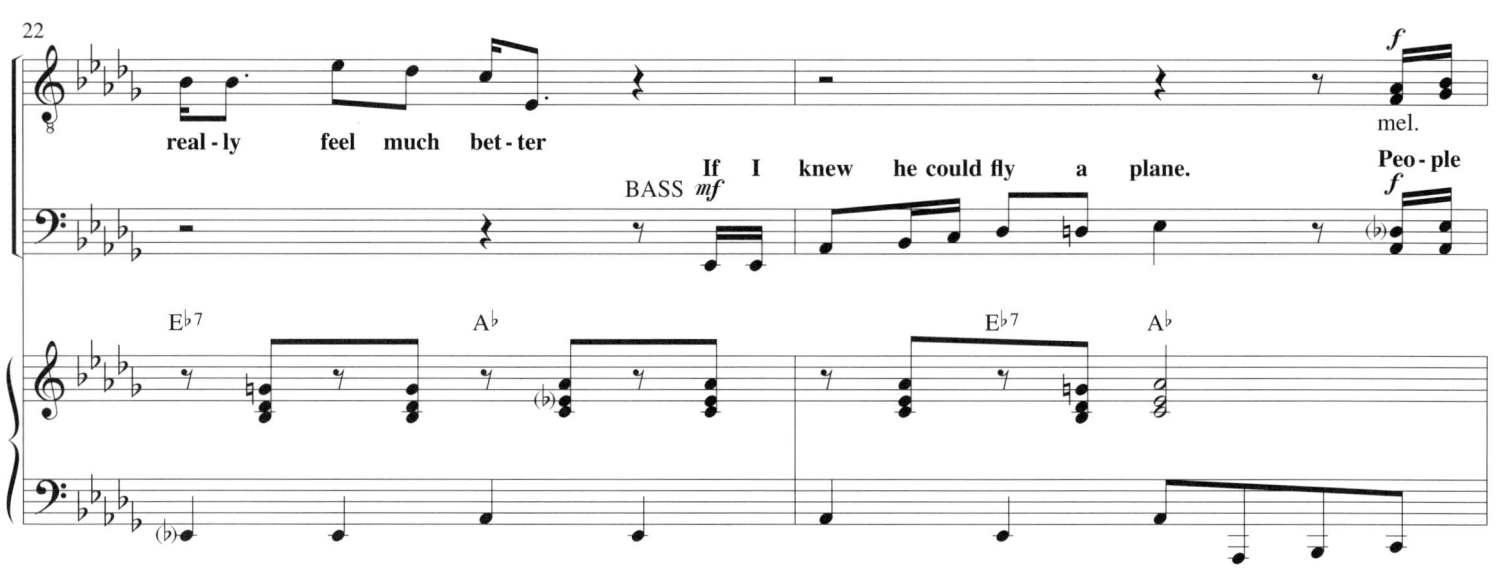

All I Want Is You
A cappella

Words and Music by
WAYNE HAUN and JOEL LINDSEY

Doo-wop feel ♩. = ca. 84

*This a cappella piece utilizes a core quartet, marked as GROUP, plus a group of soloists, featuring seven voices all together. When soloists are not singing, they may double their singing parts in the GROUP.

© 2006 Christian Taylor Music (BMI), a div. of Daywind Music (admin. by EverGreen Copyrights)/
New Spring Publishing (ASCAP)/ Vacation Boy Music (ASCAP) (All rights on behalf of Vacation Boy Music
administered by New Spring Publishing.)/Sunset Gallery Music (BMI). All rights reserved. Used by permission.

PLEASE NOTE: Copying of this product is NOT covered by CCLI licenses. For CCLI information call 1-800-234-2446.

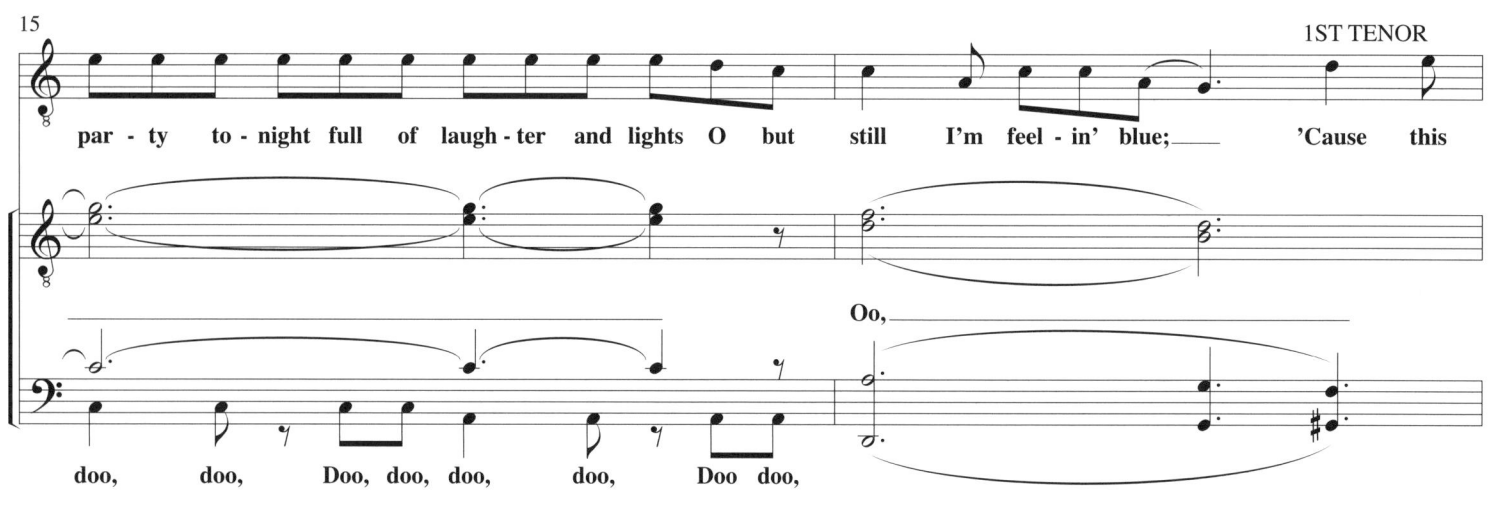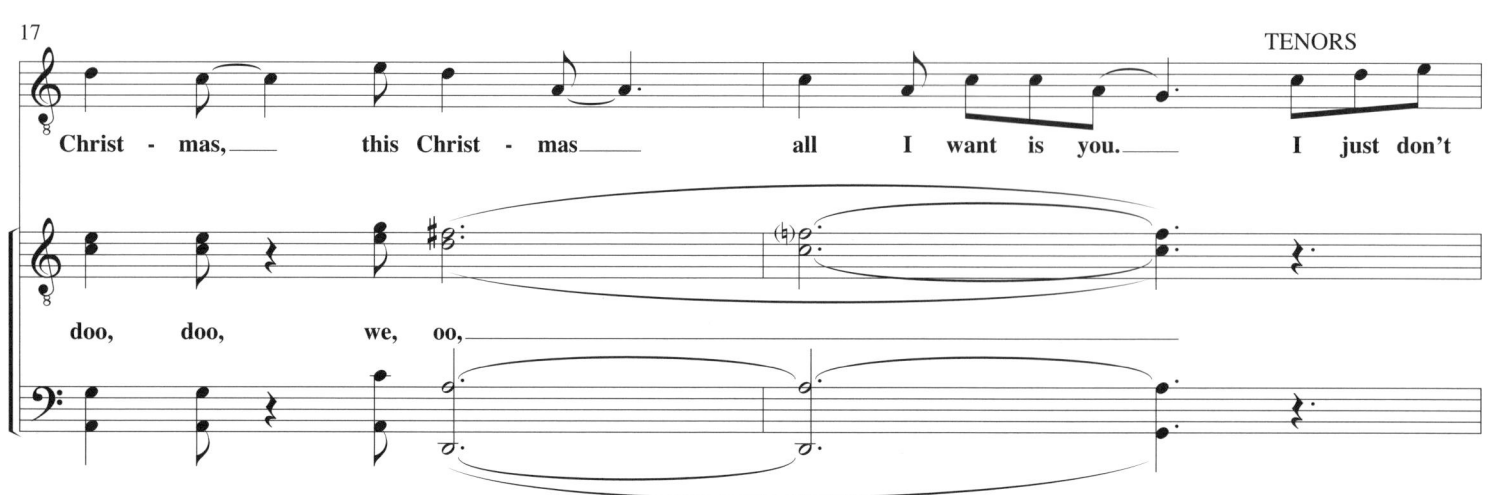

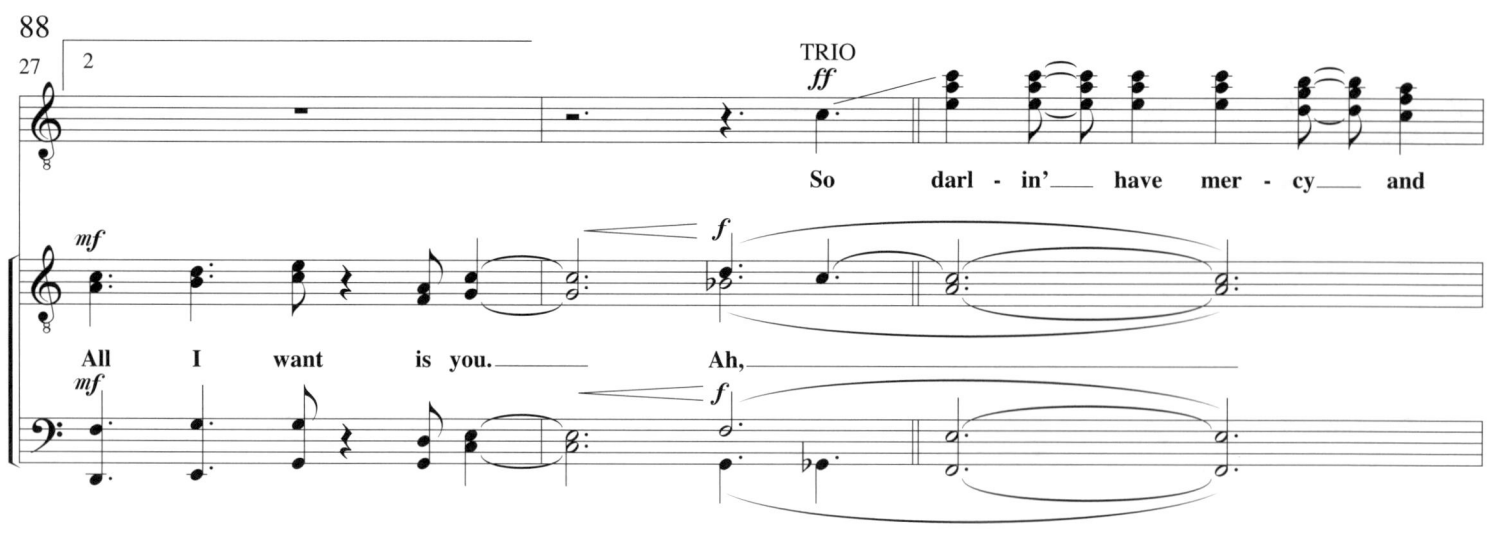

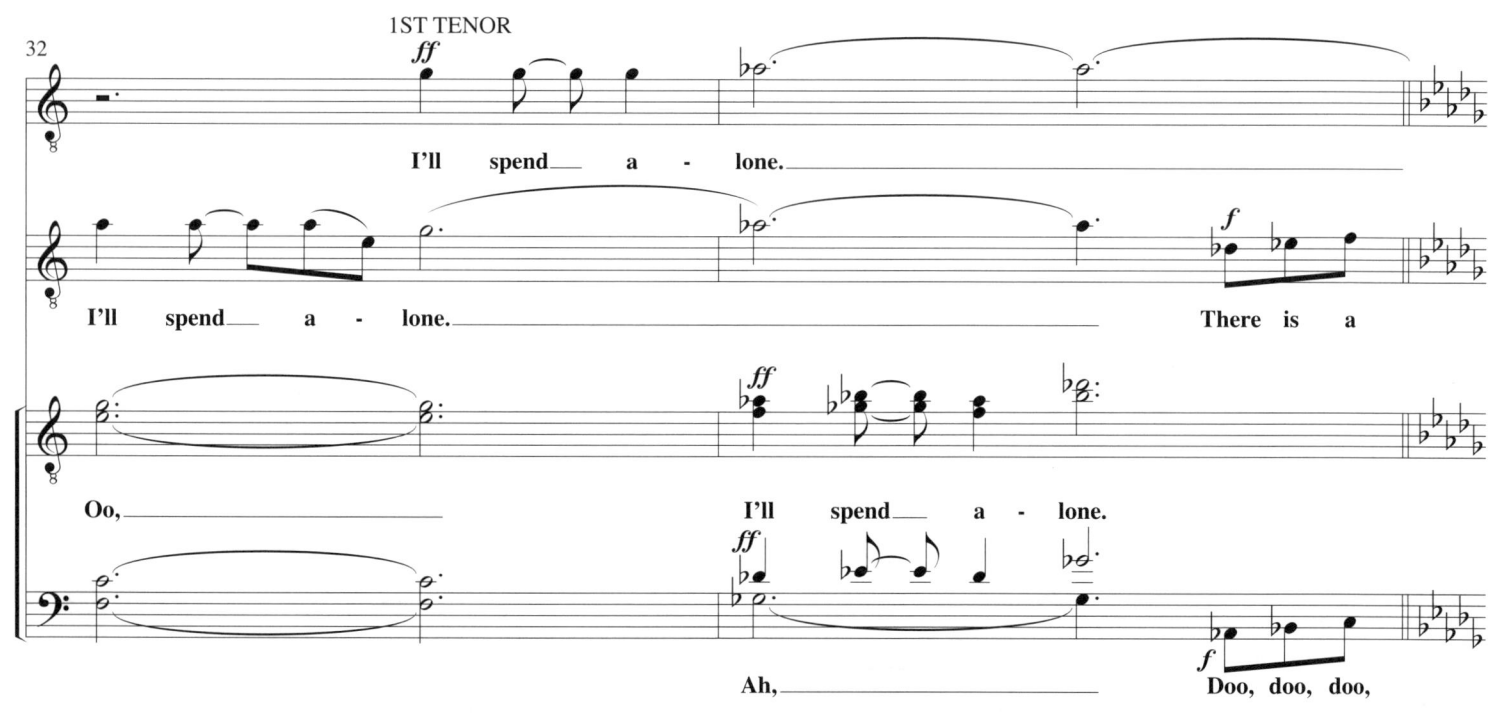

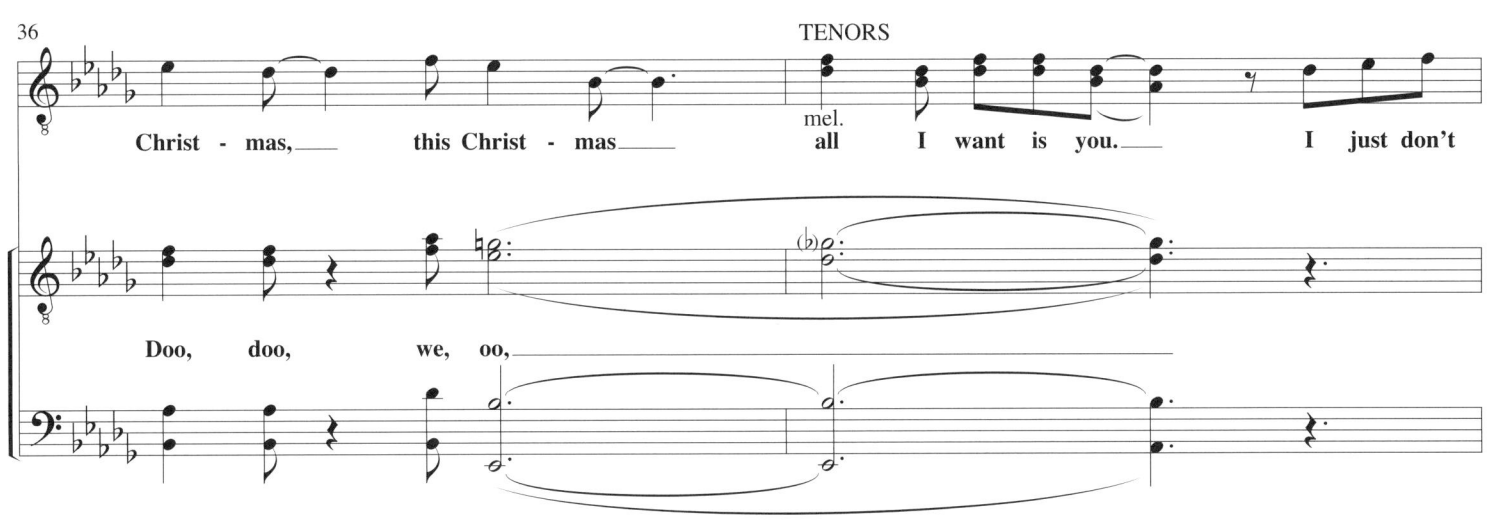

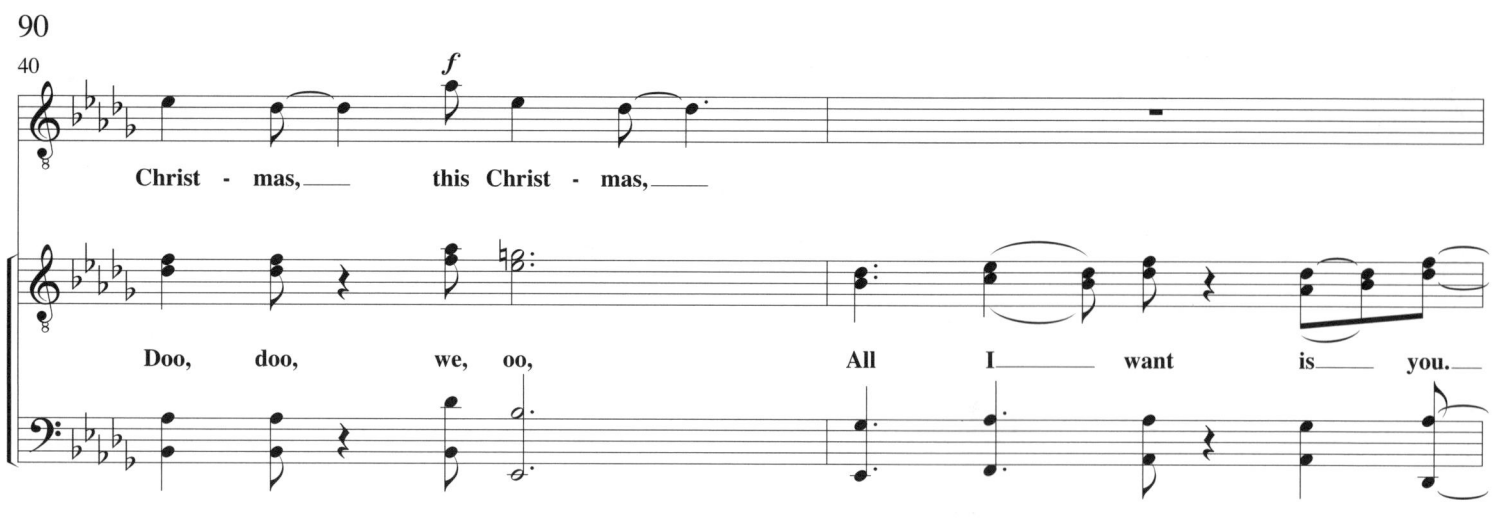

Christmas in Indiana

GLORIA GAITHER

BENJAMIN GAITHER

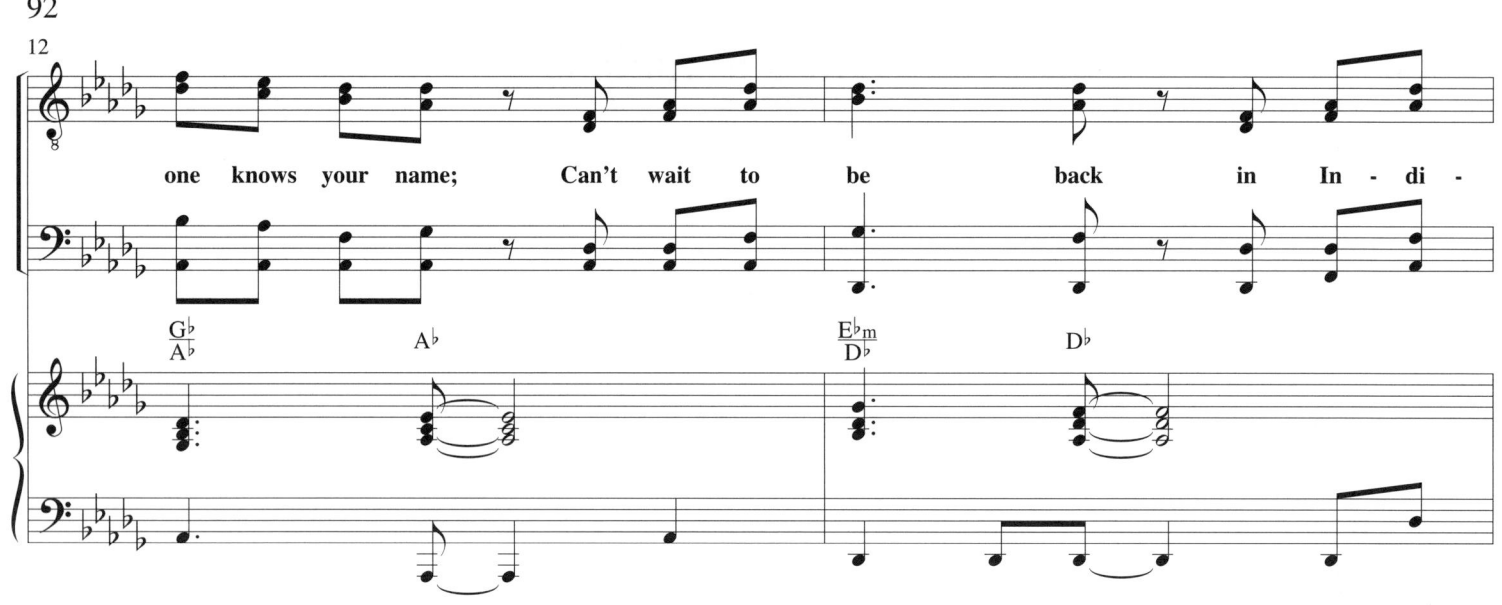

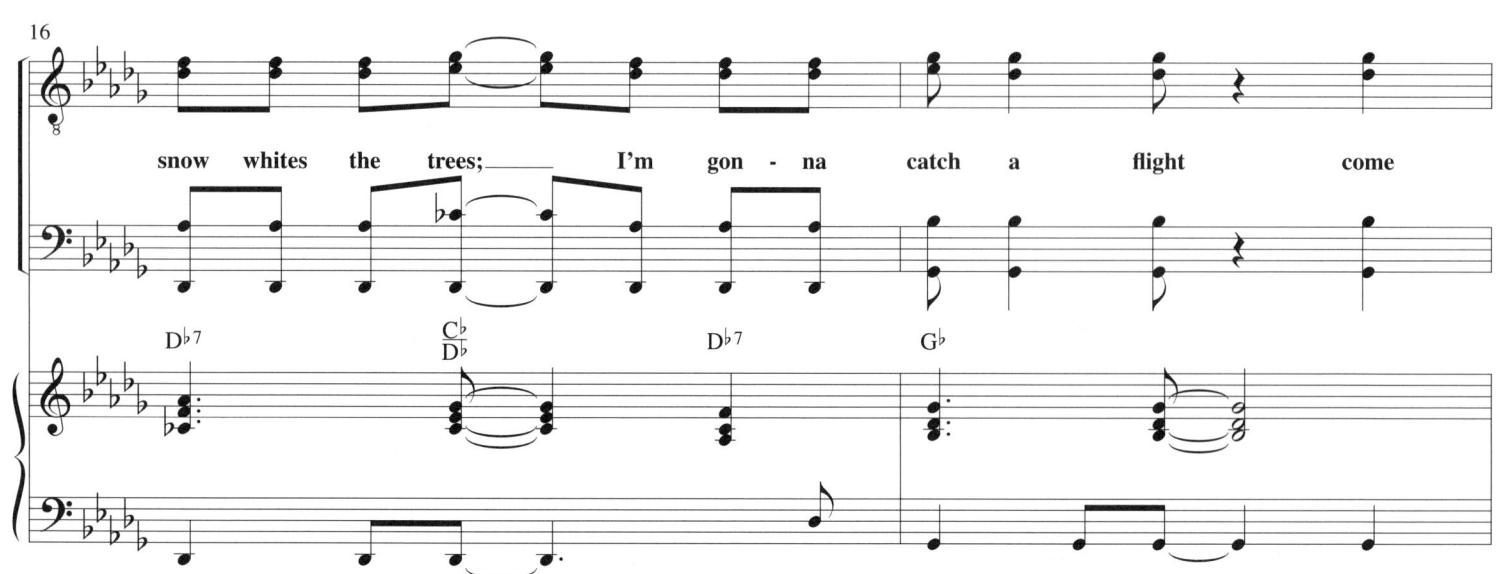

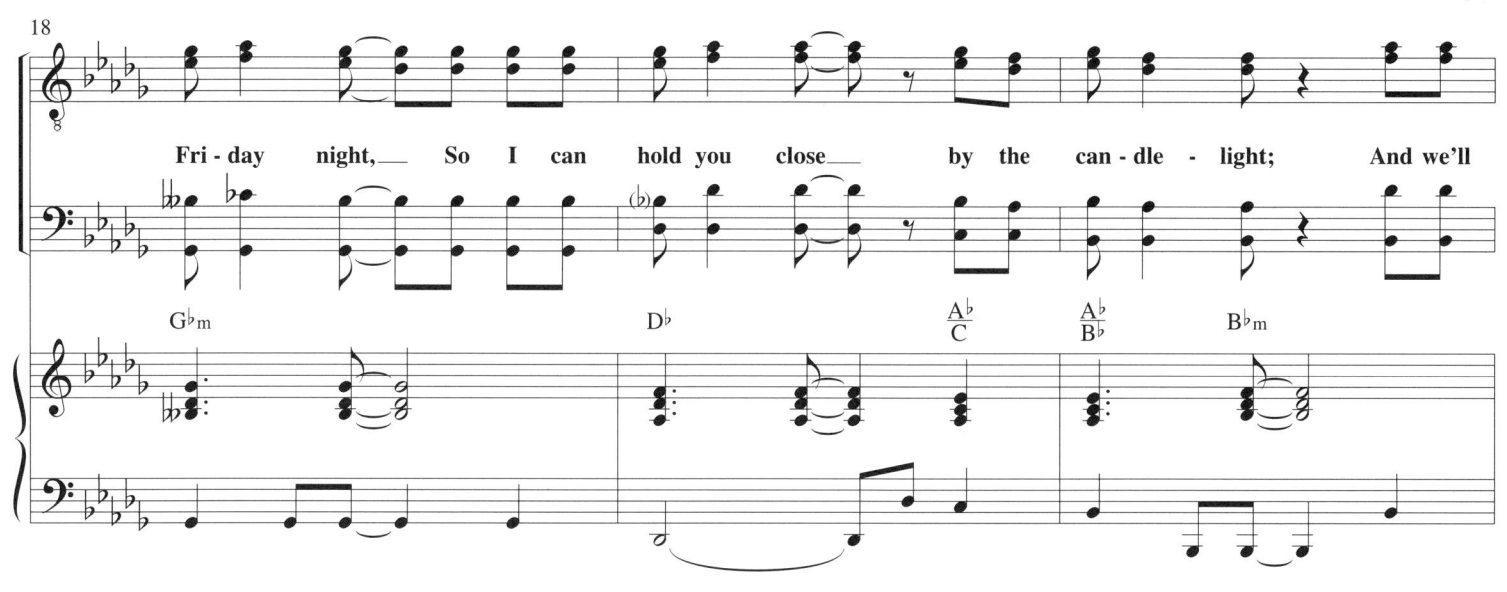
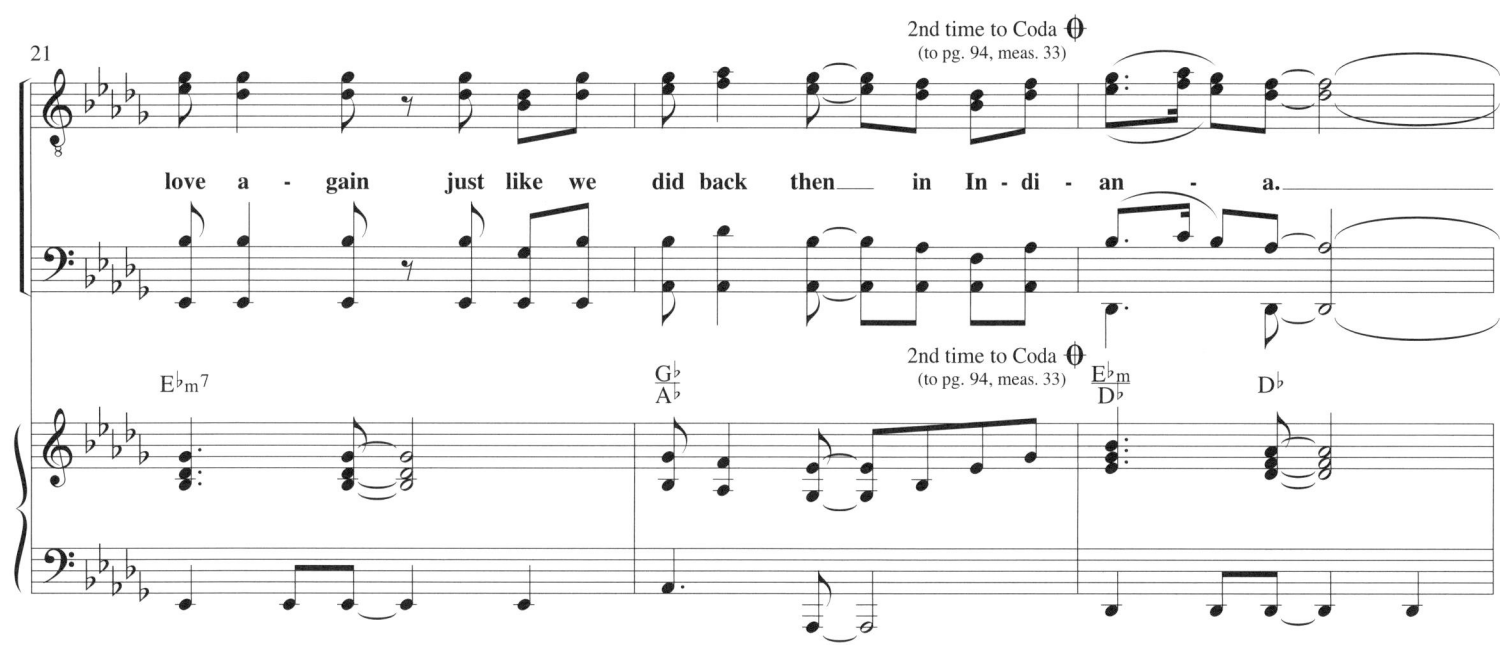
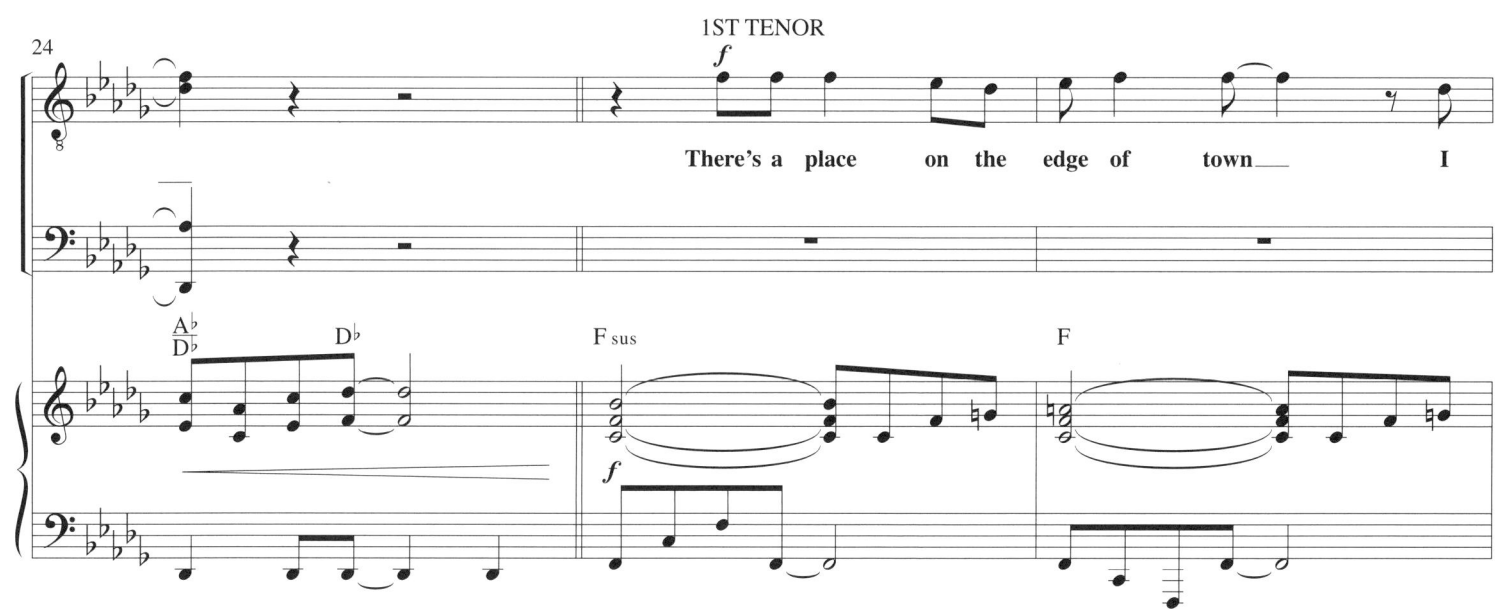

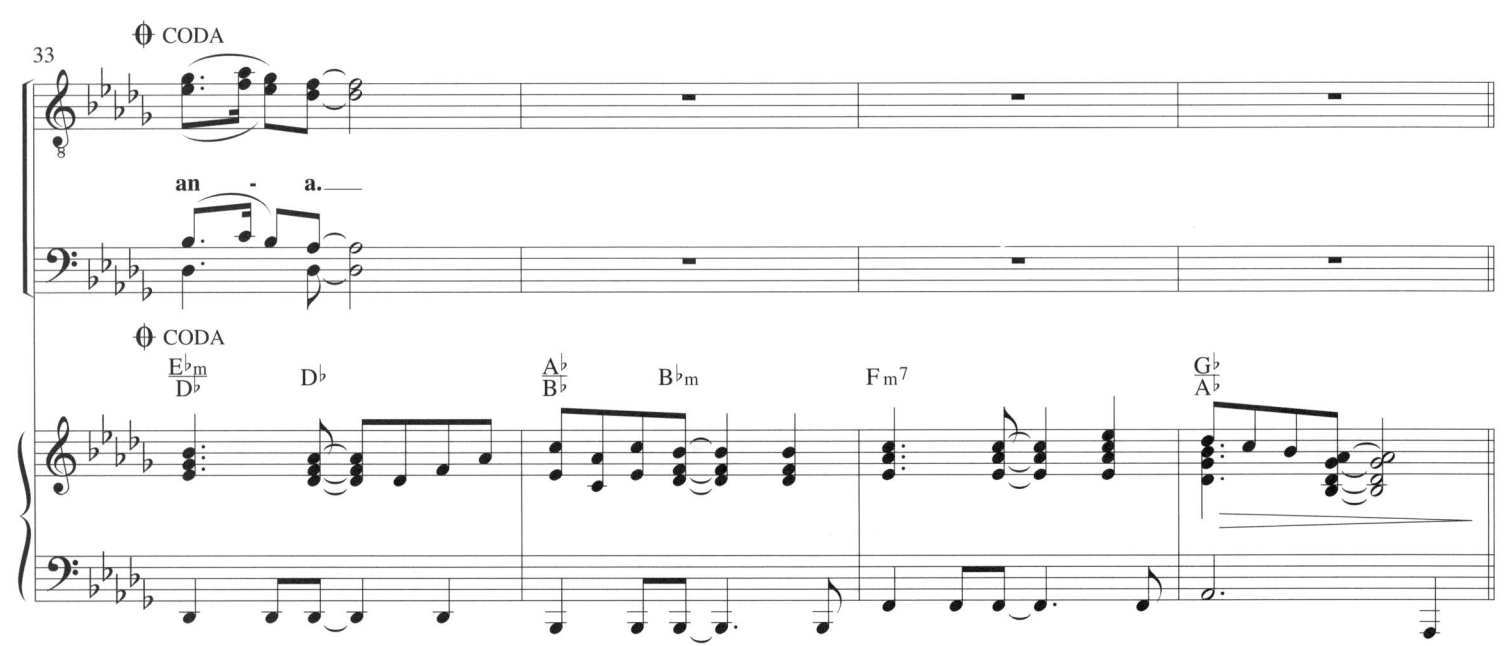

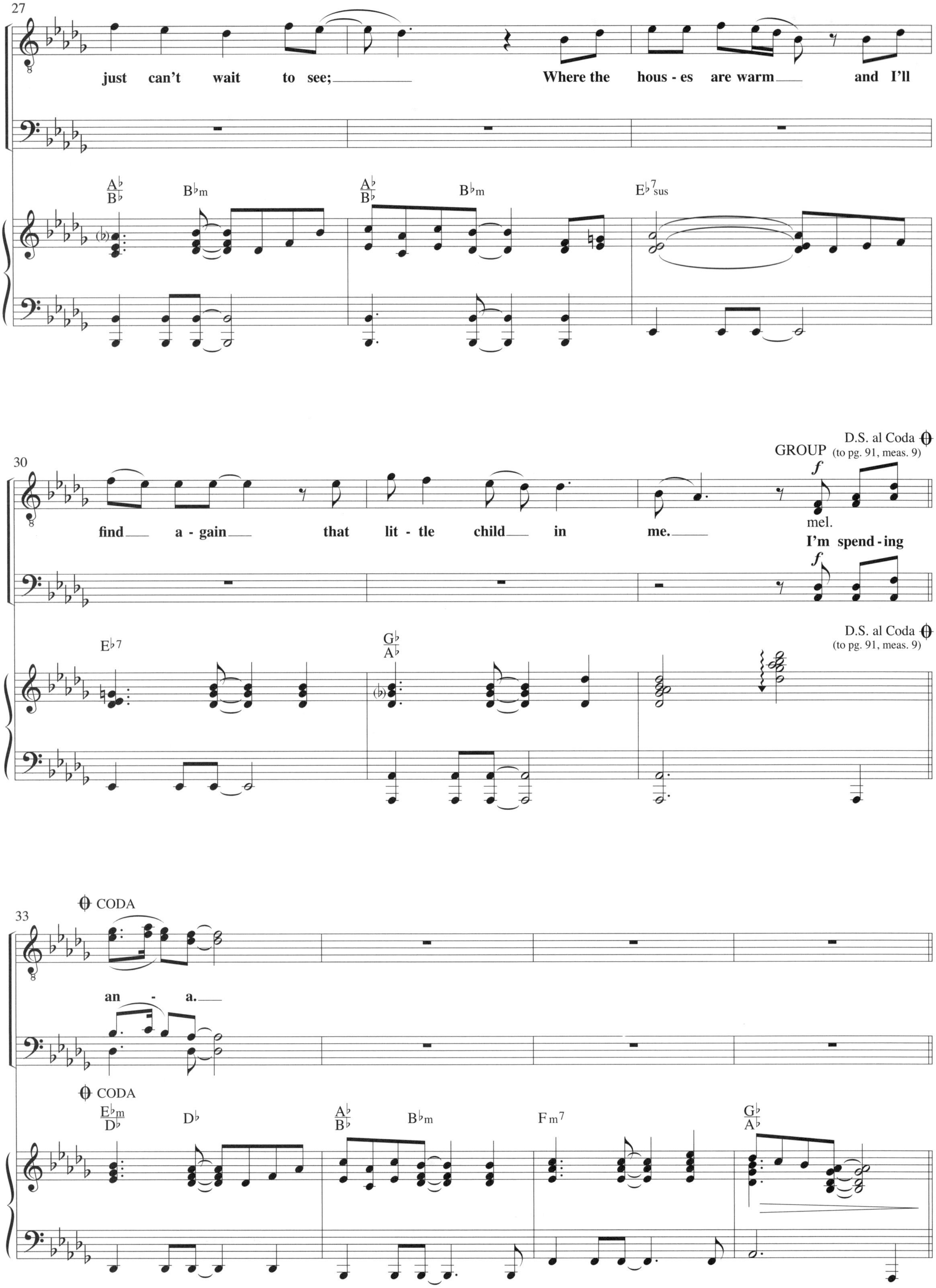
27
just can't wait to see; Where the hous - es are warm and I'll
A♭/B♭ B♭m A♭/B♭ B♭m E♭7sus
30
find a - gain that lit - tle child in me.
GROUP
mel.
I'm spend - ing
D.S. al Coda (to pg. 91, meas. 9)
E♭7 G♭/A♭
D.S. al Coda (to pg. 91, meas. 9)
33
CODA
an - a.
CODA
E♭m/D♭ D♭ A♭/B♭ B♭m Fm7 G♭/A♭

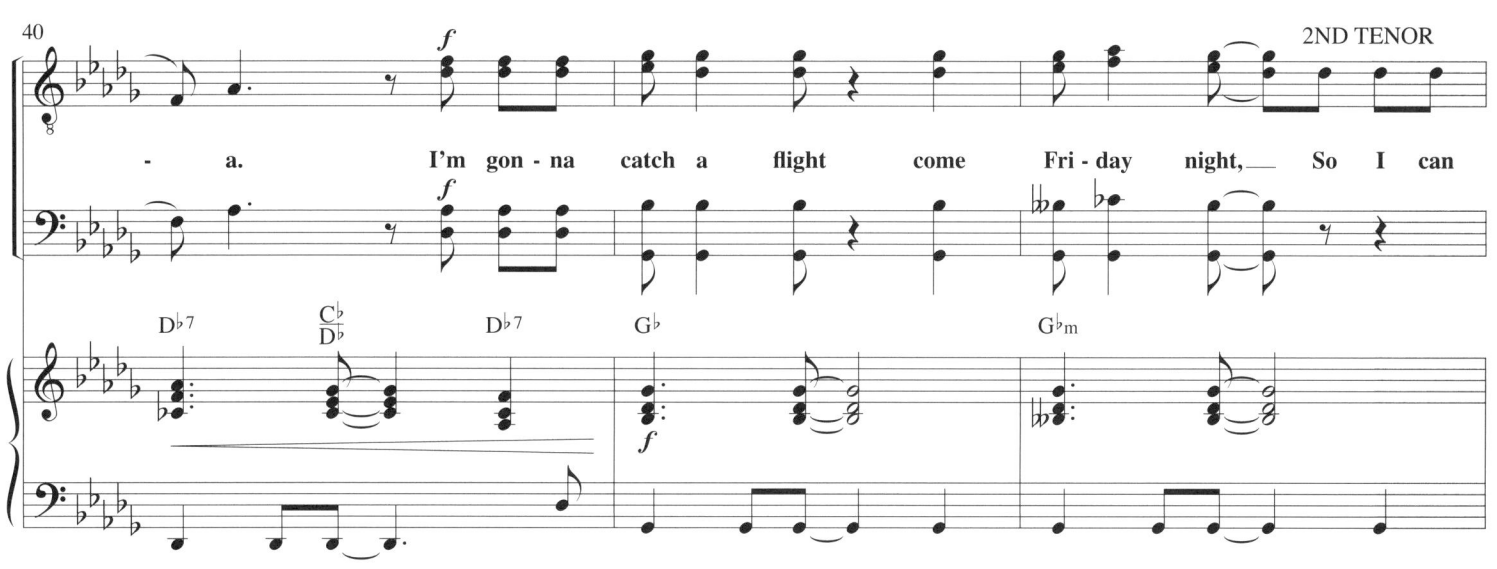

97

Silent Night! Holy Night!

JOSEPH MOHR

FRANZ GRUBER

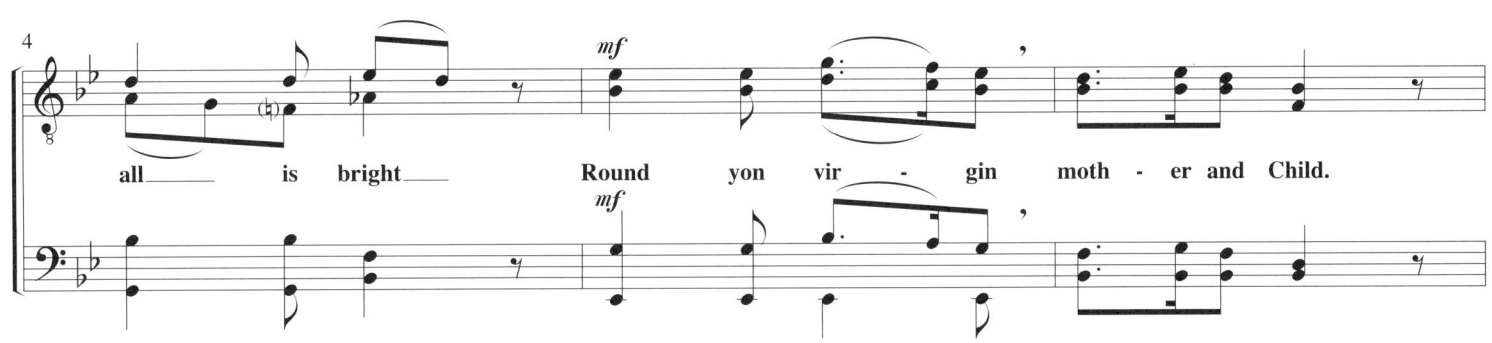

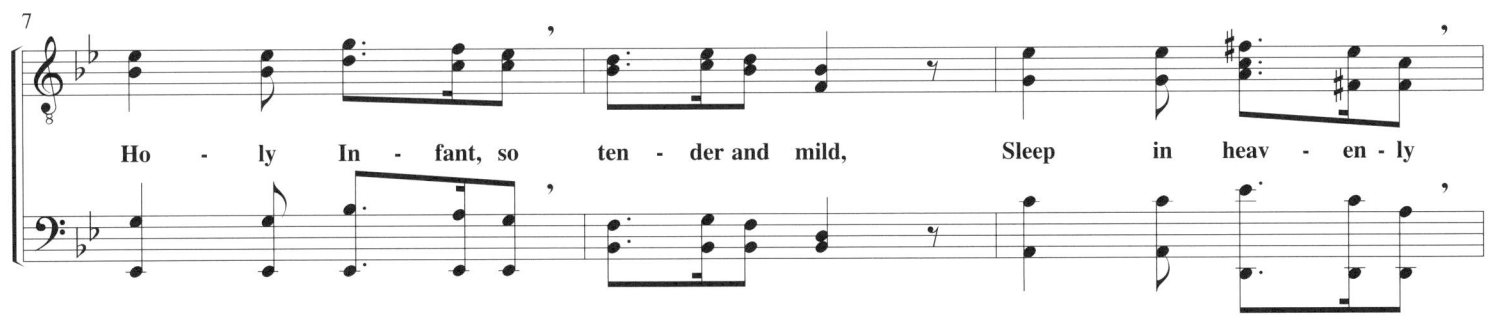

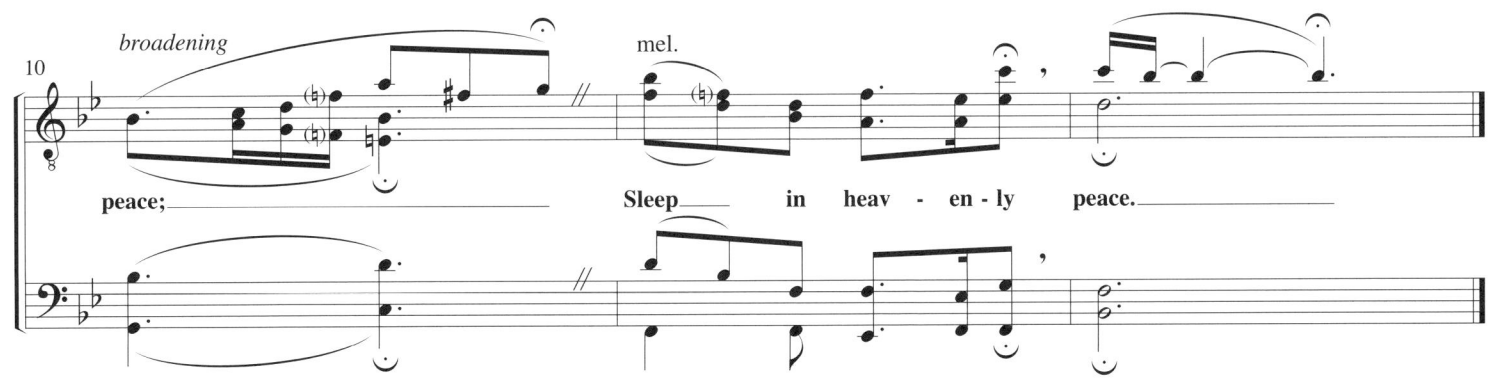

Arr. © 2009 PsalmSinger Music (BMI) (Administered by The Copyright Company)/
Ernie Sig Sound Music (BMI). All rights reserved.

PLEASE NOTE: Copying of this product is NOT covered by CCLI licenses. For CCLI information call 1-800-234-2446.

Light a Candle

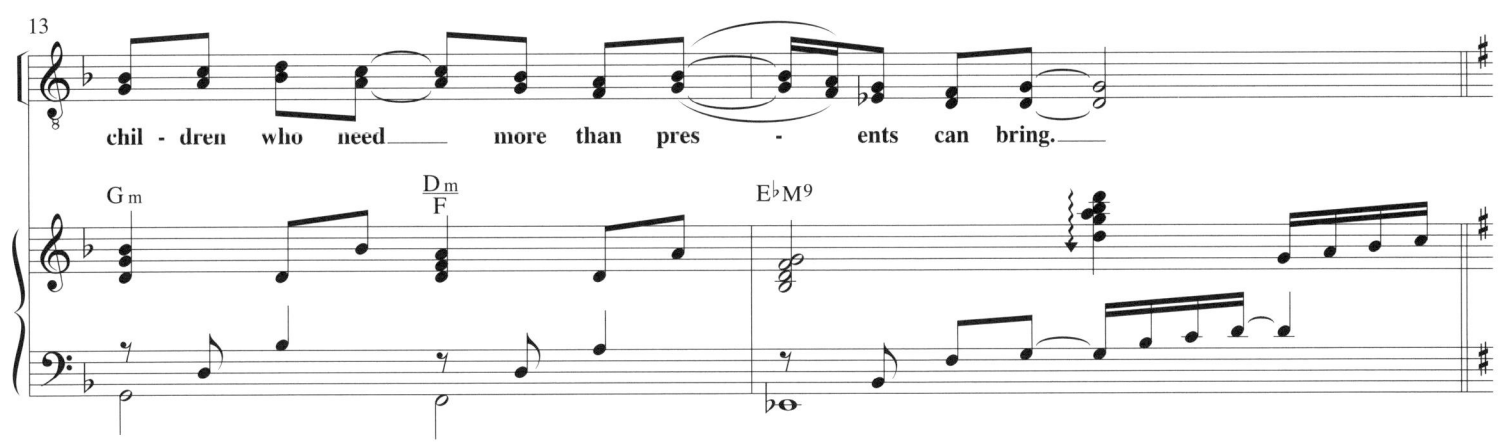

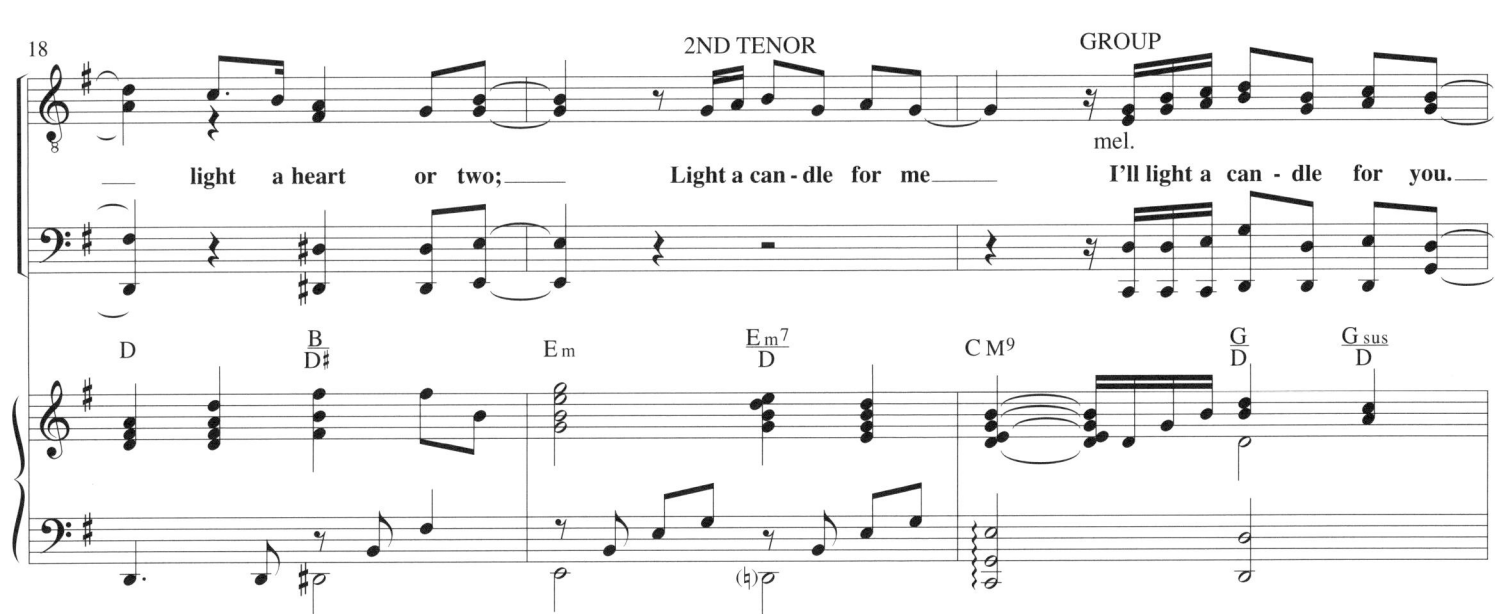

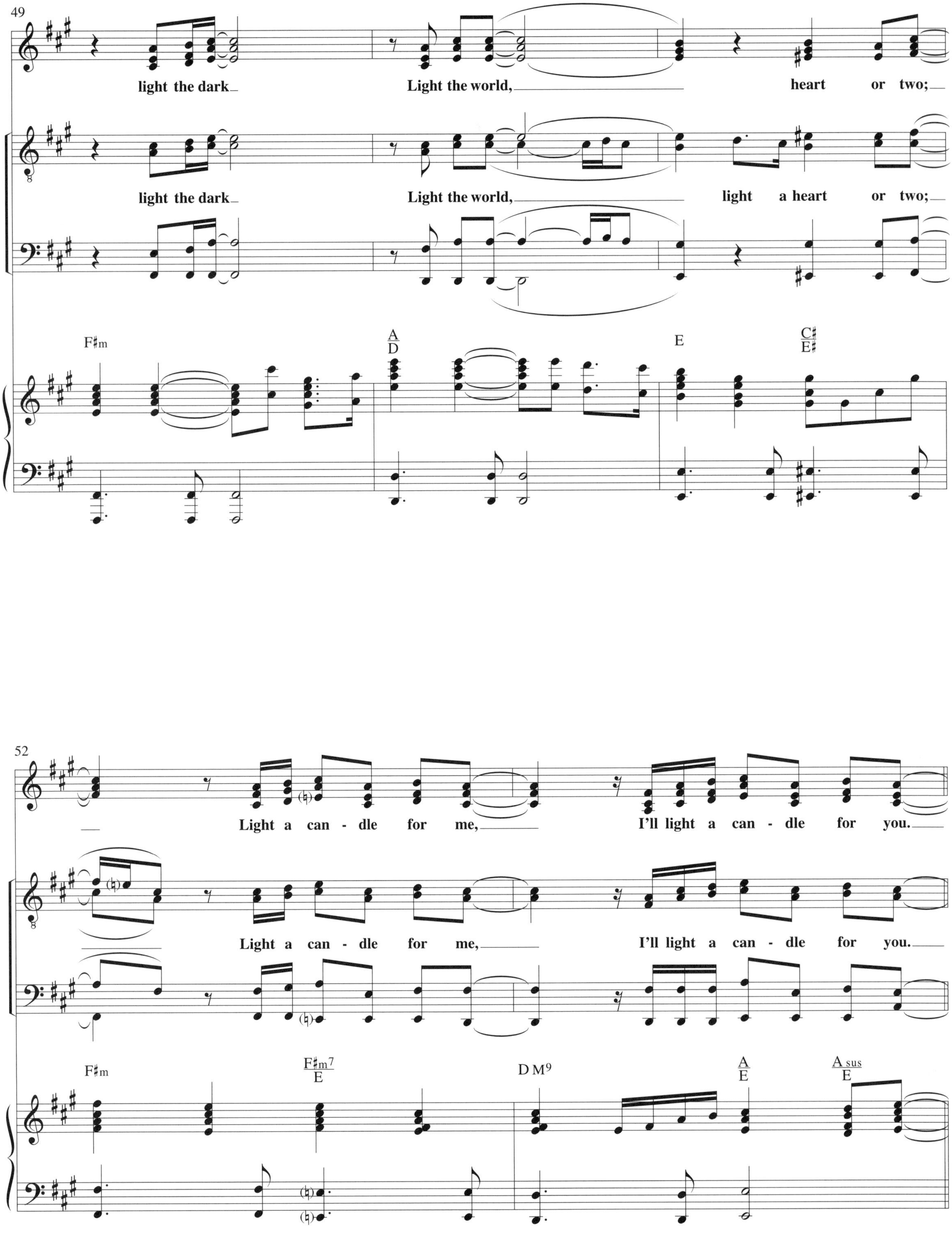
49
light the dark
Light the world,
heart or two;
light the dark
Light the world,
light a heart or two;
F♯m
A/D
E
C♯/E♯
52
Light a can - dle for me,
I'll light a can - dle for you.
Light a can - dle for me,
I'll light a can - dle for you.
F♯m
F♯m7/E
D M9
A/E
A sus/E

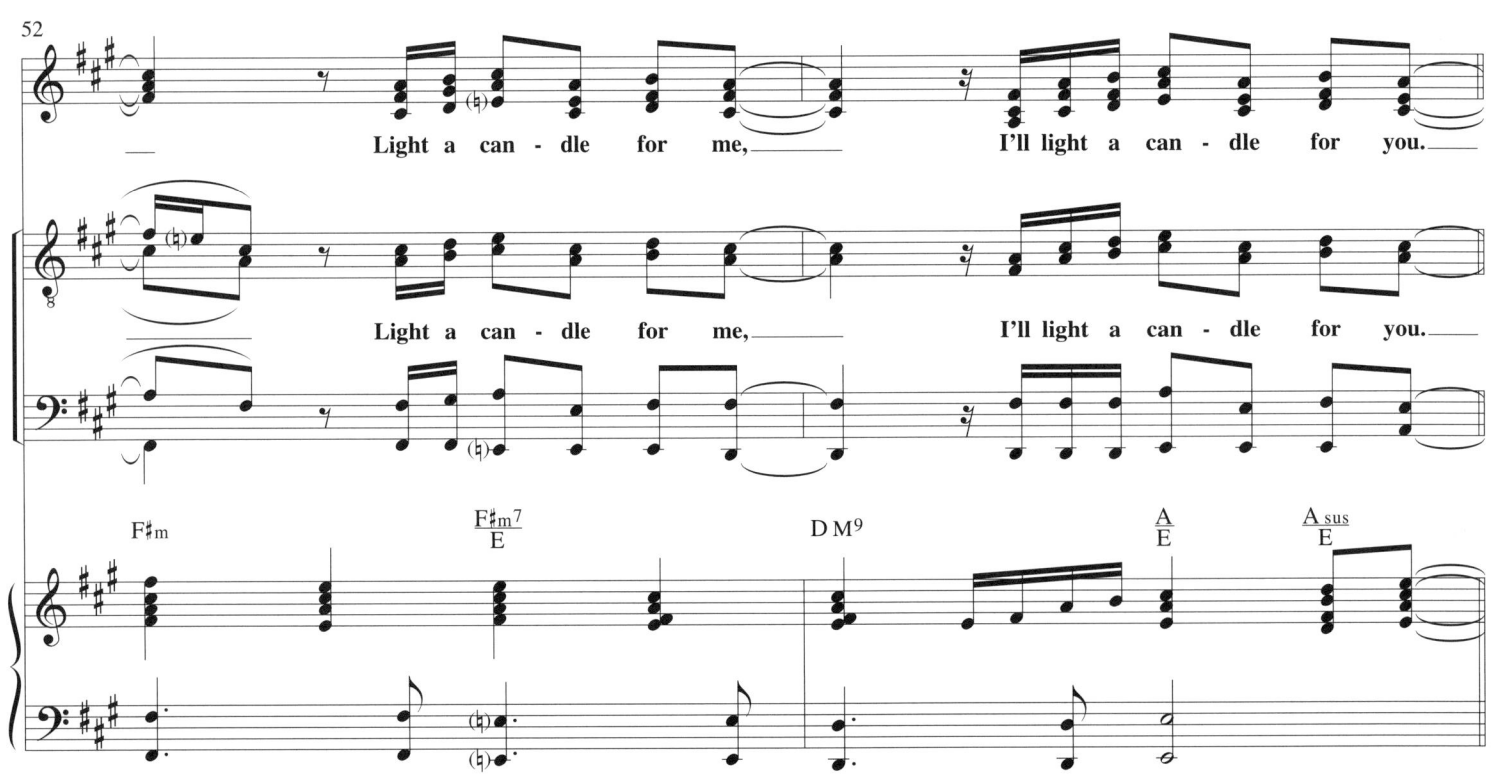

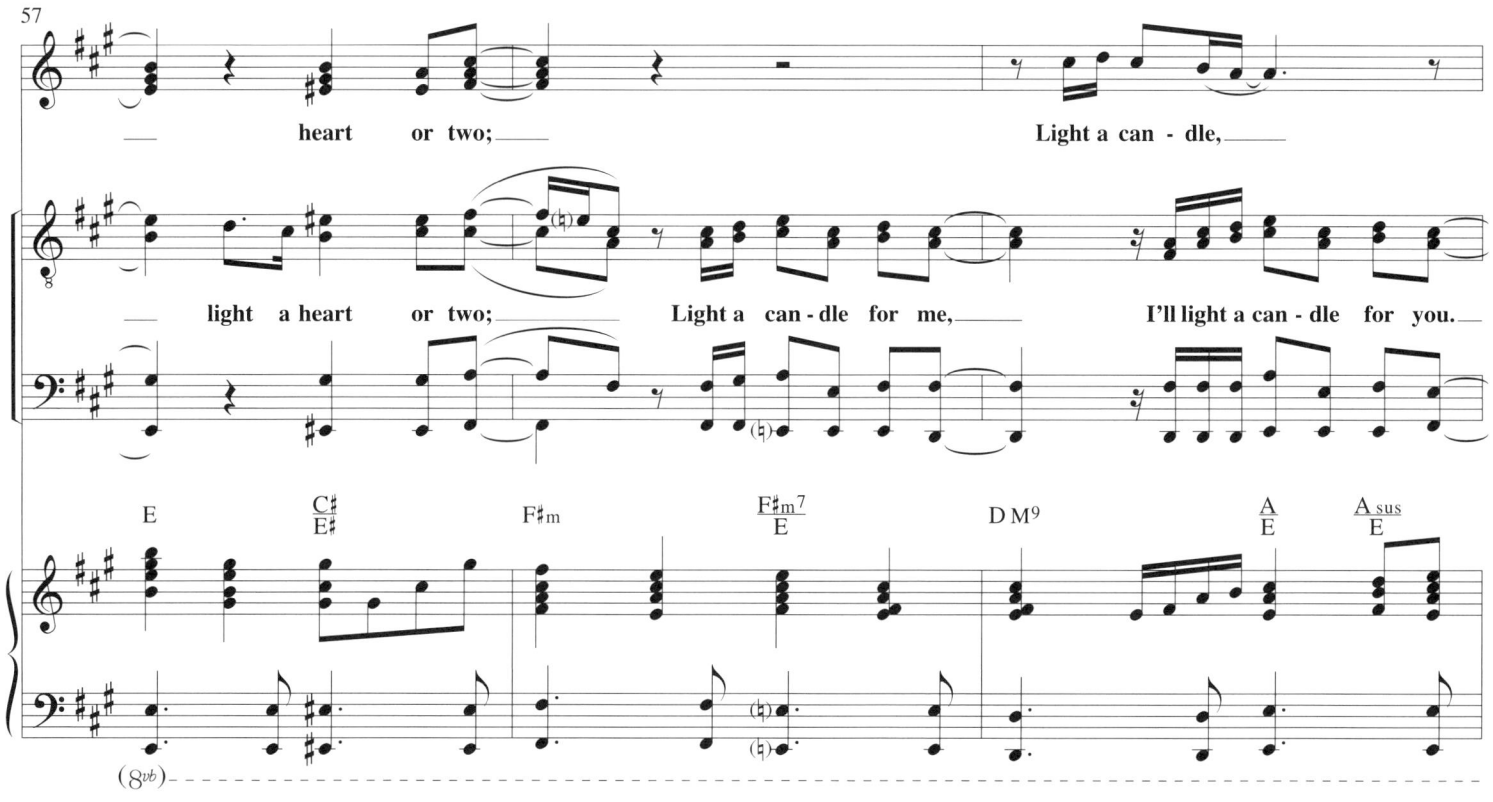

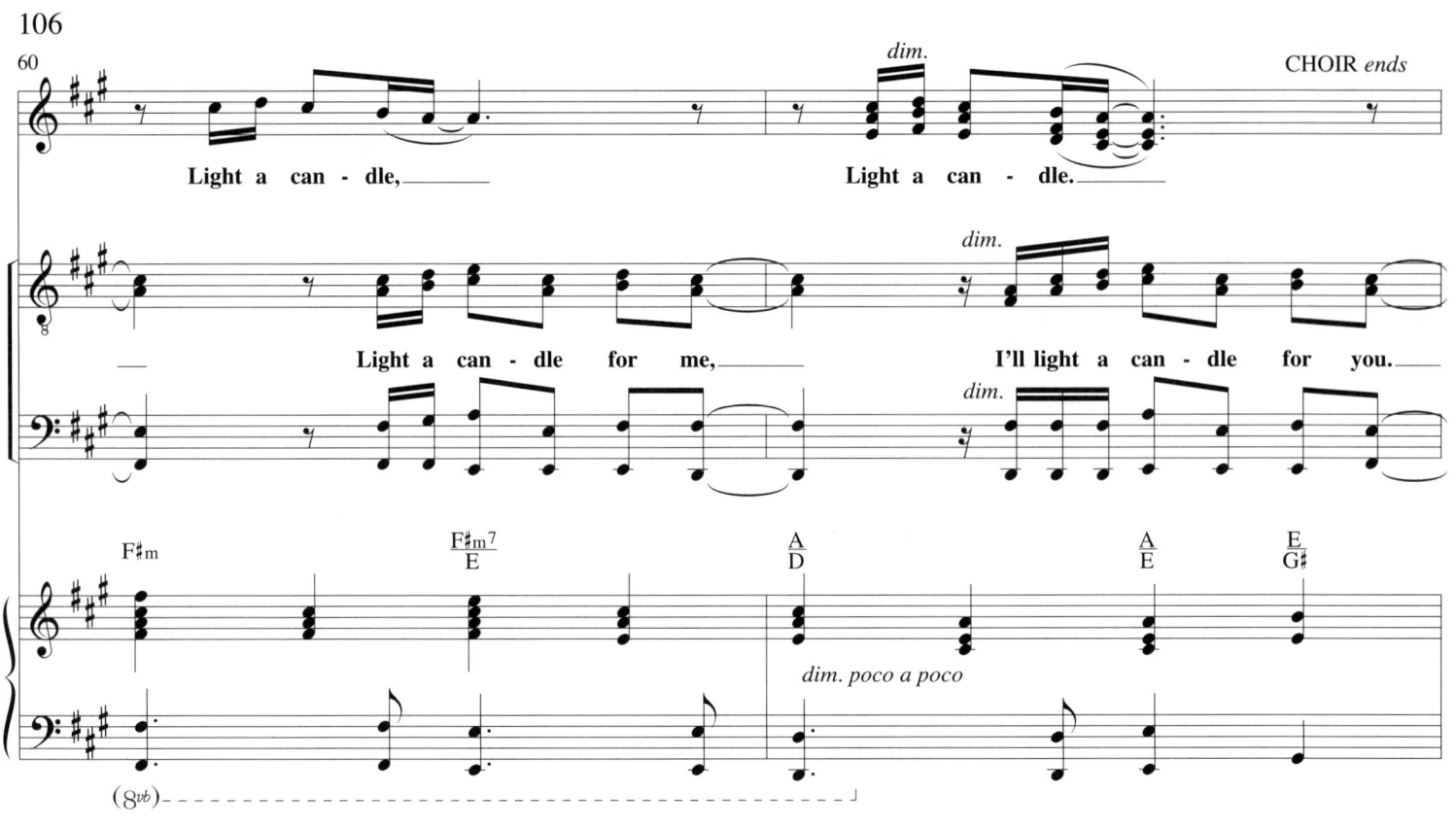
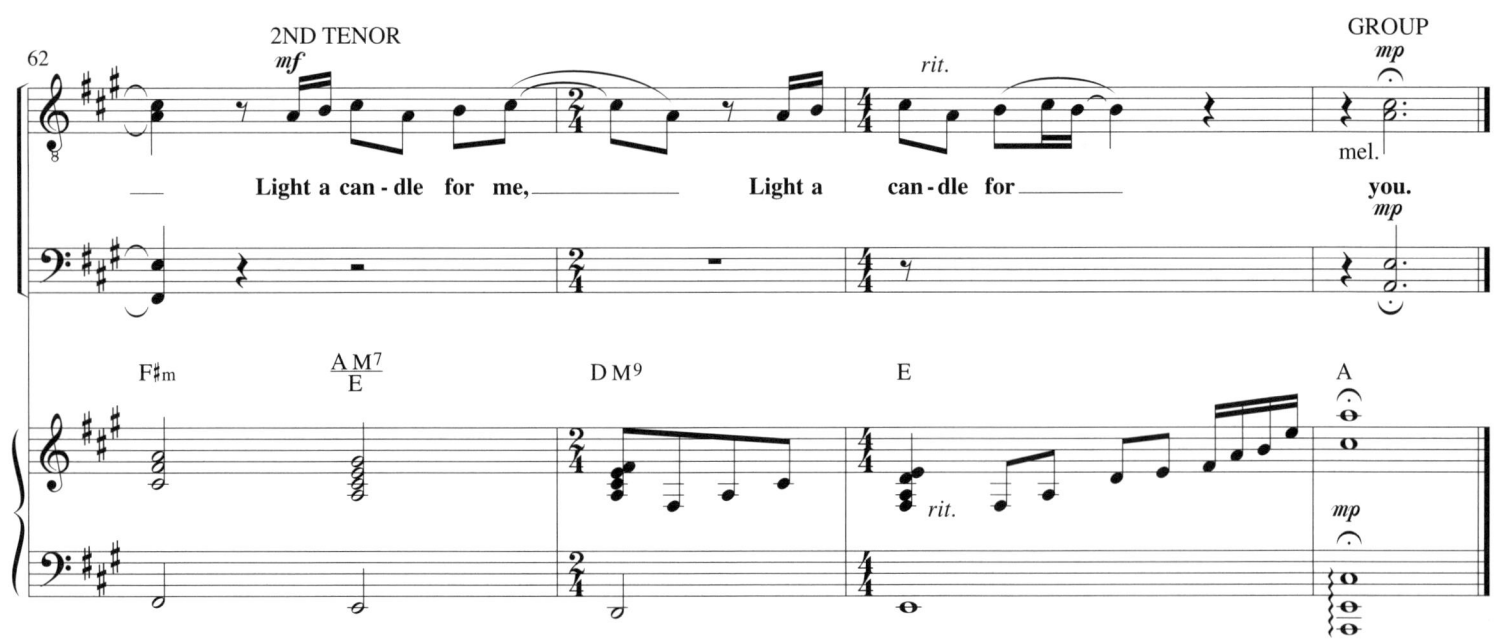

Amen

108

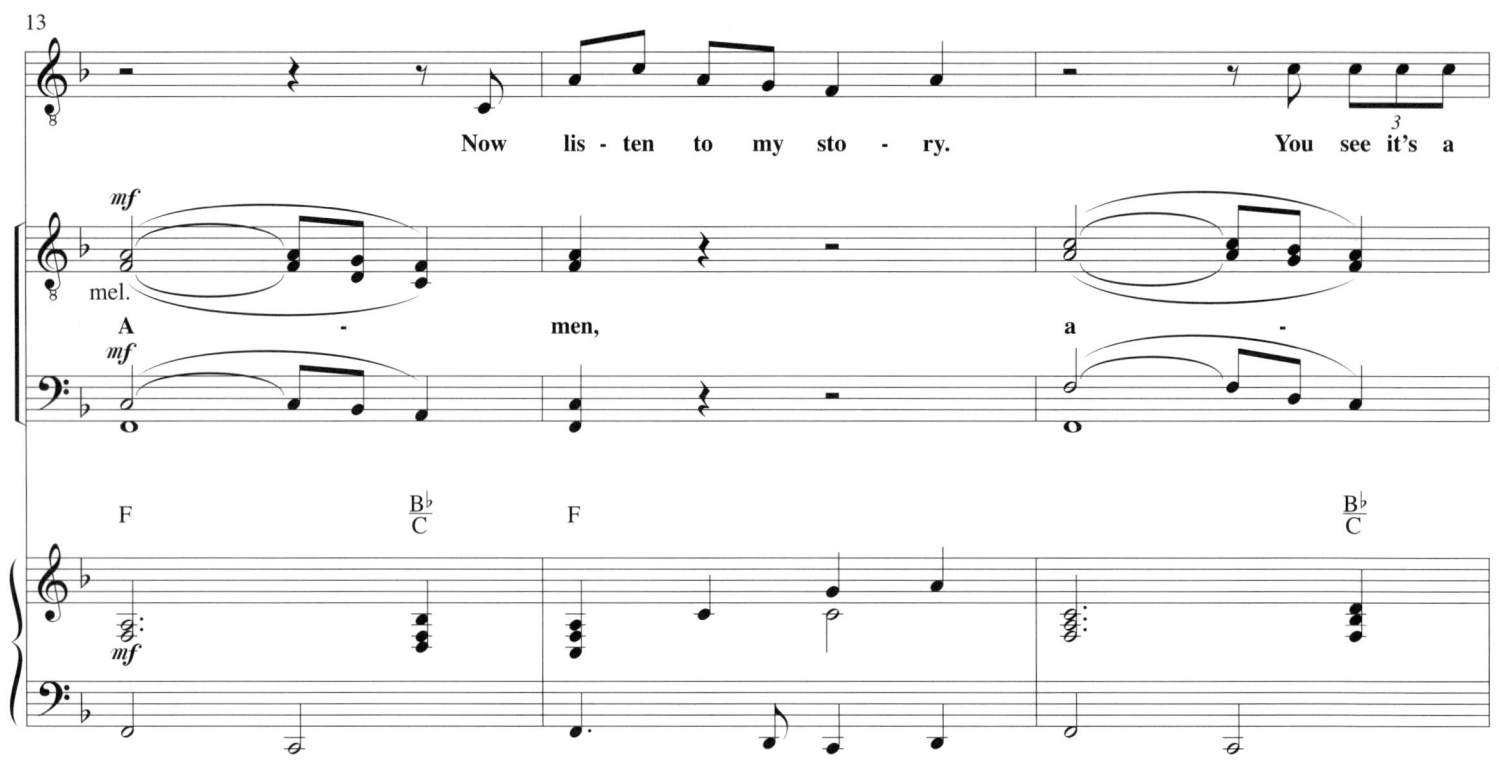

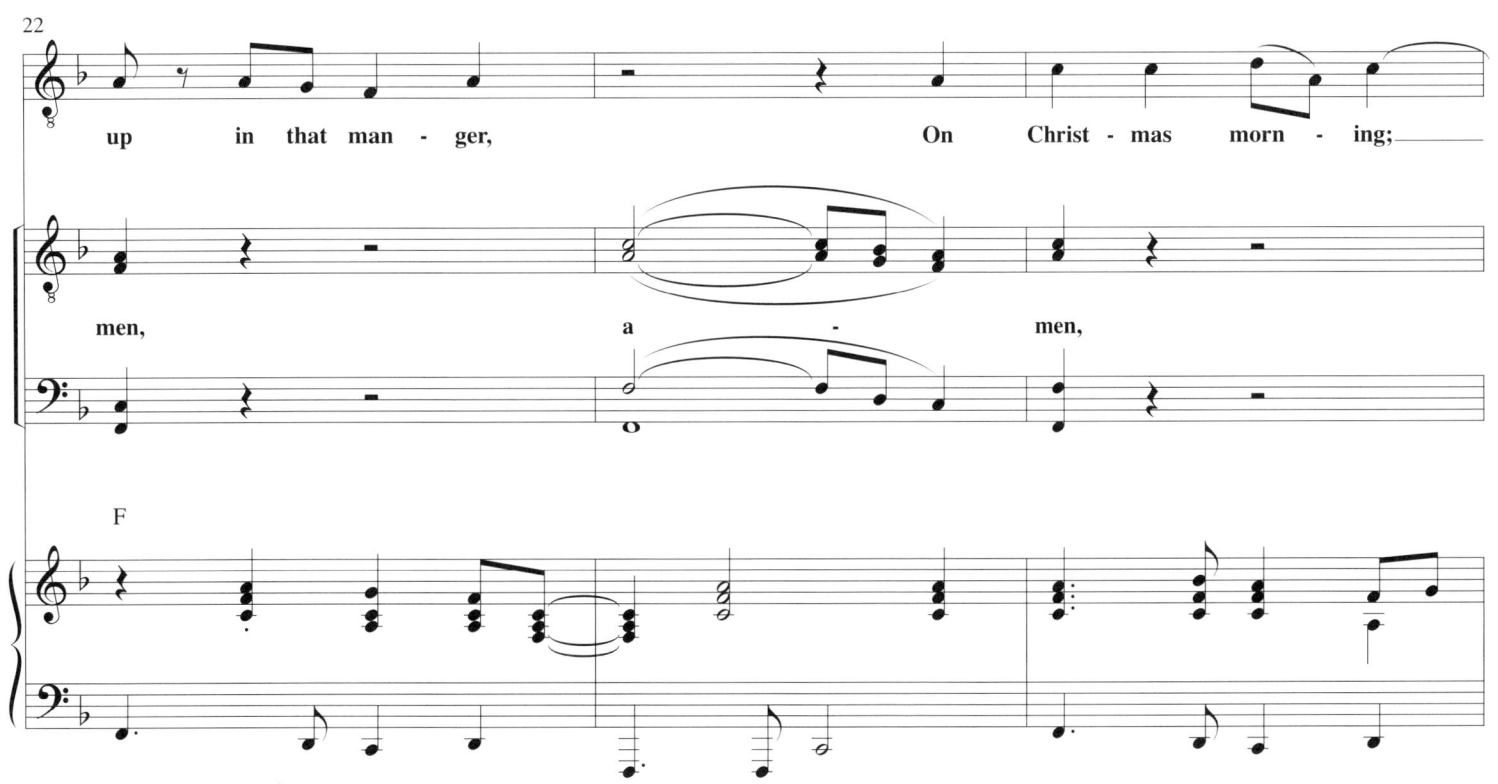

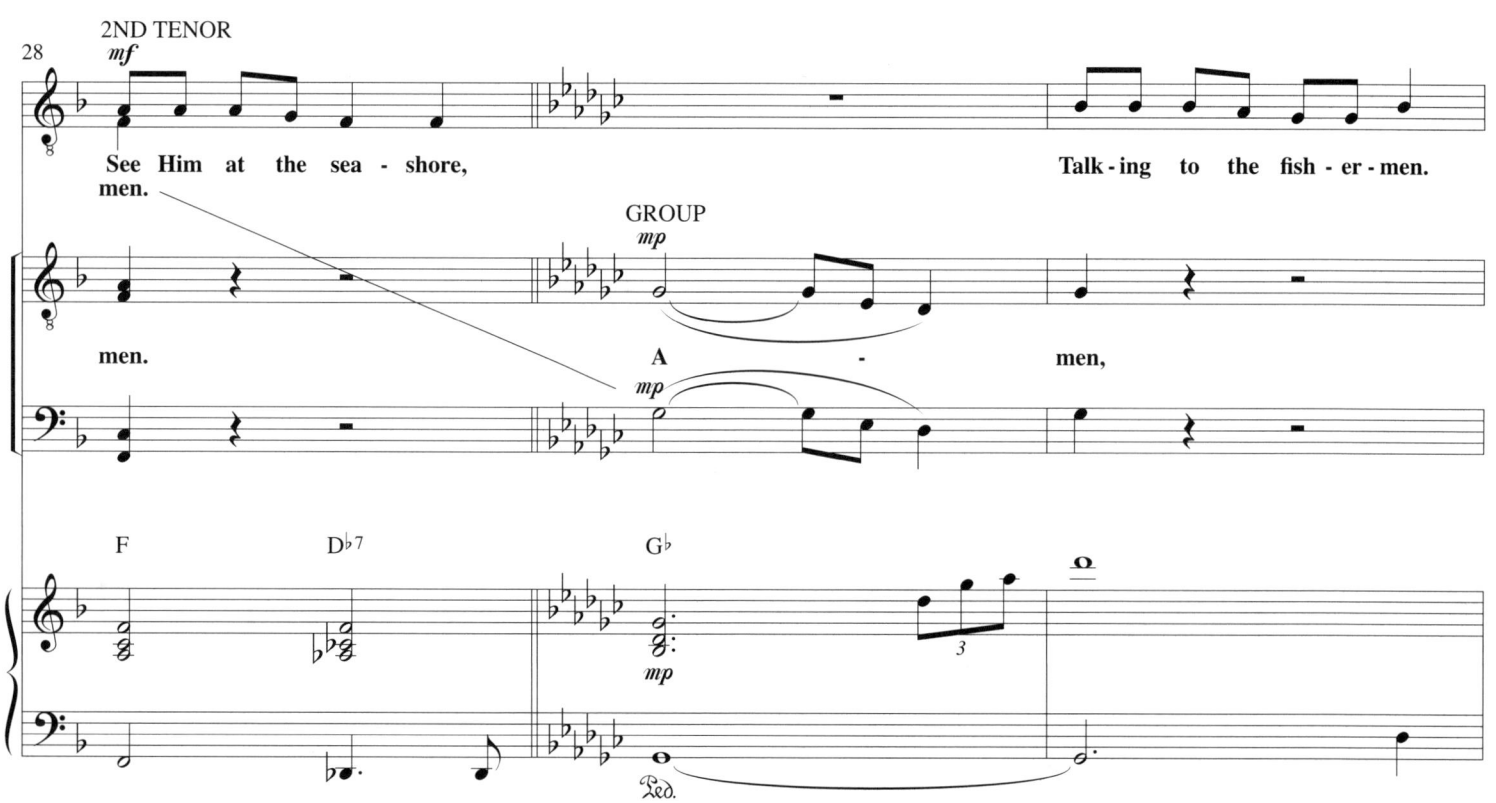

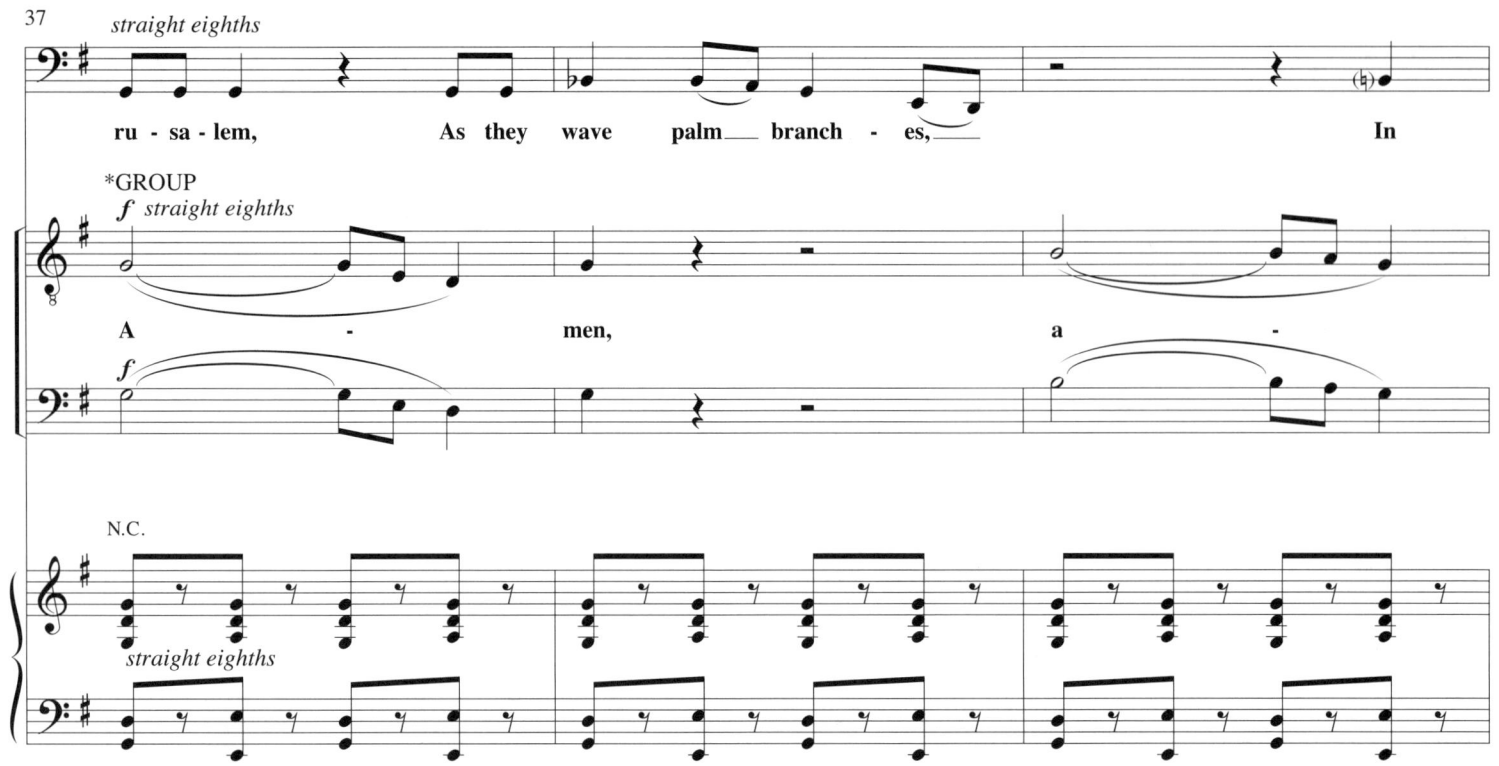
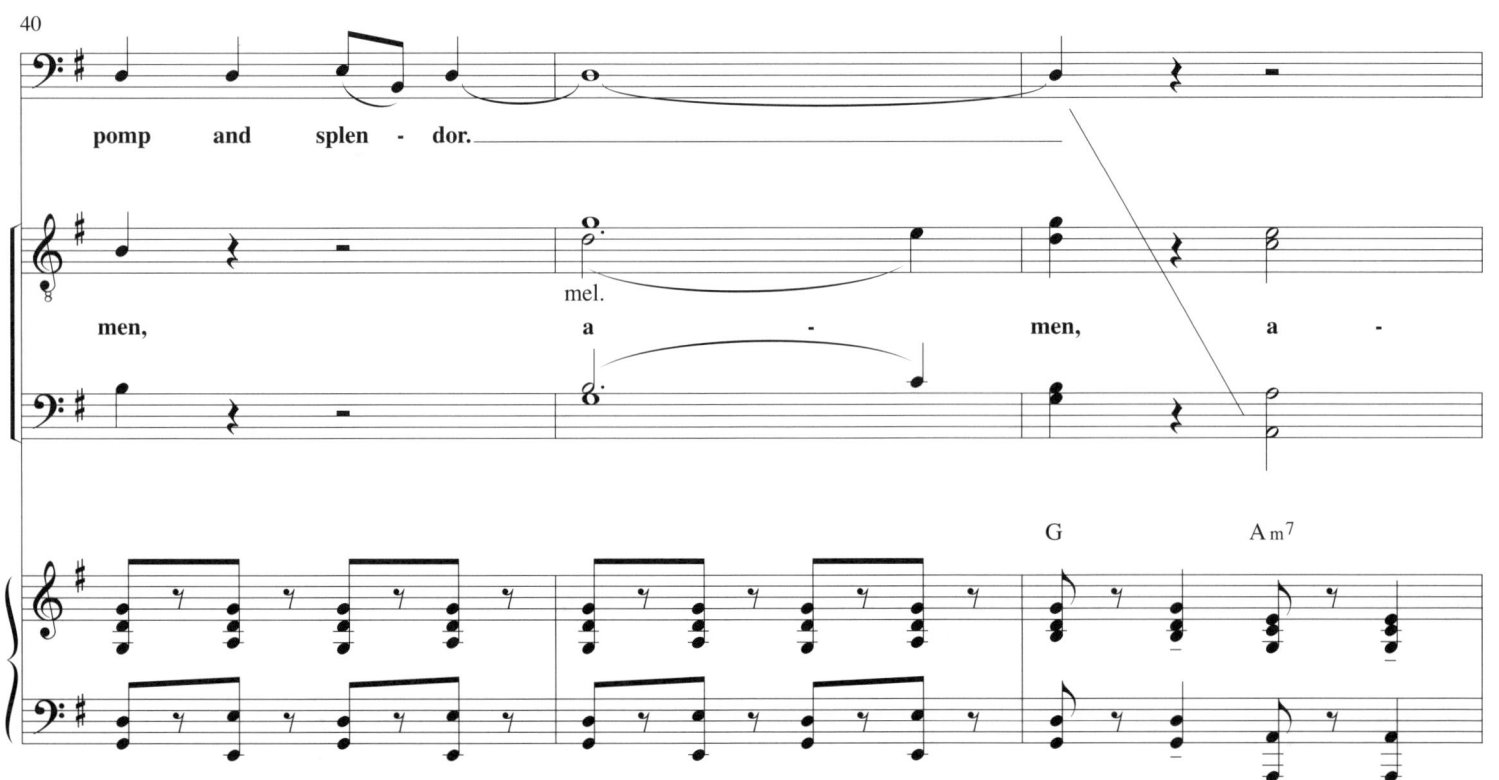

*Optional Choir may double the Group parts from here to the end.

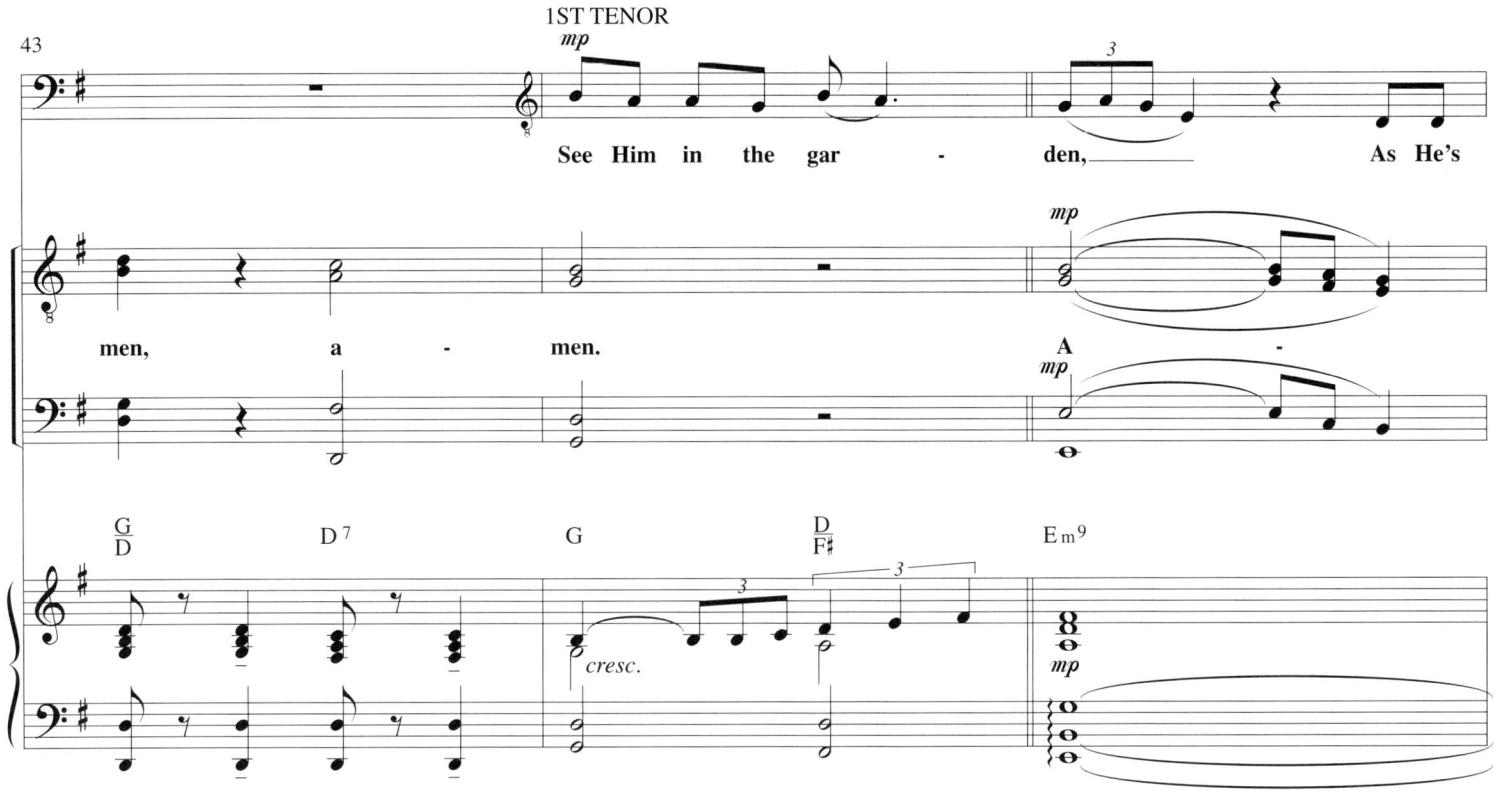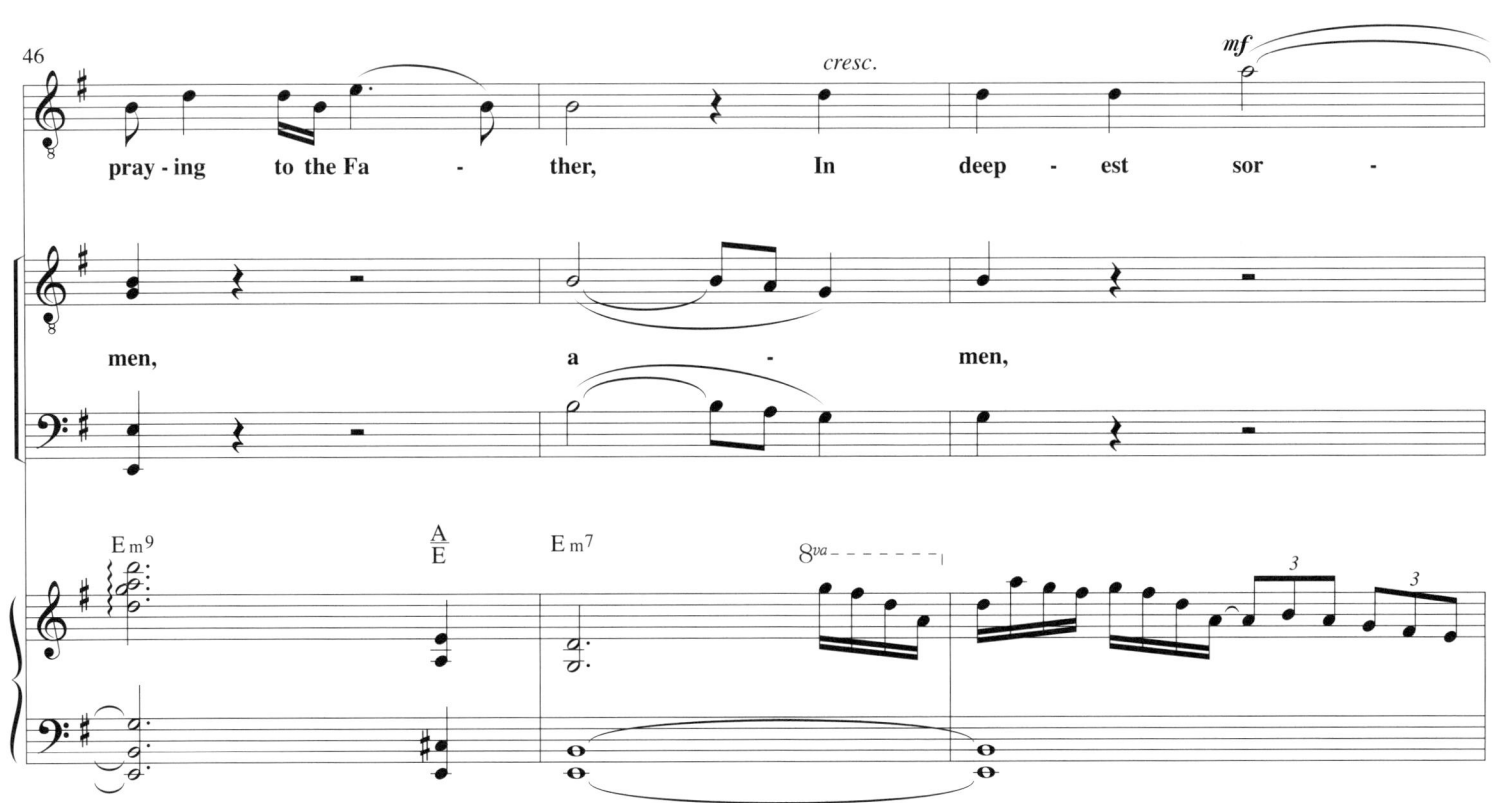

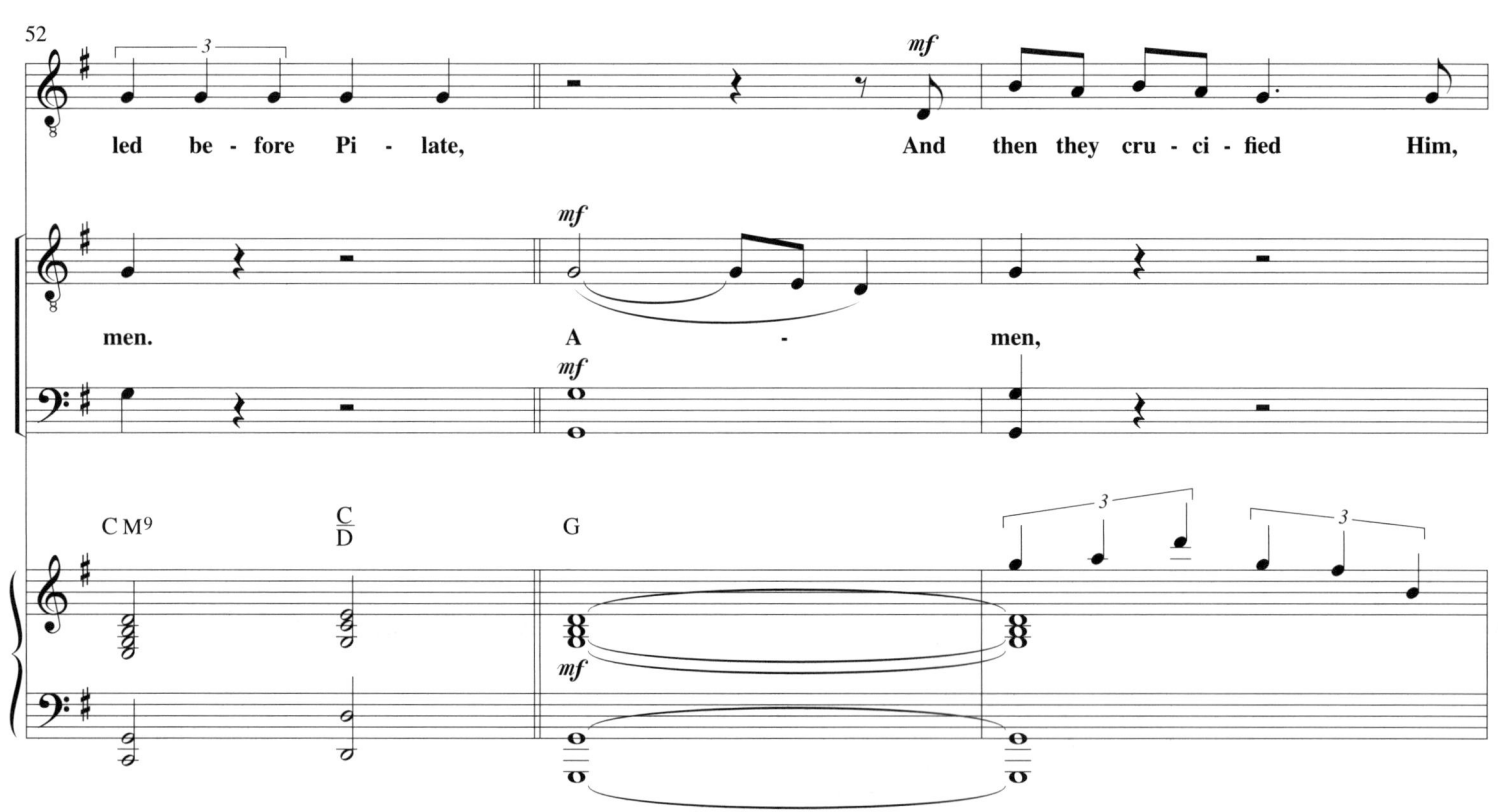

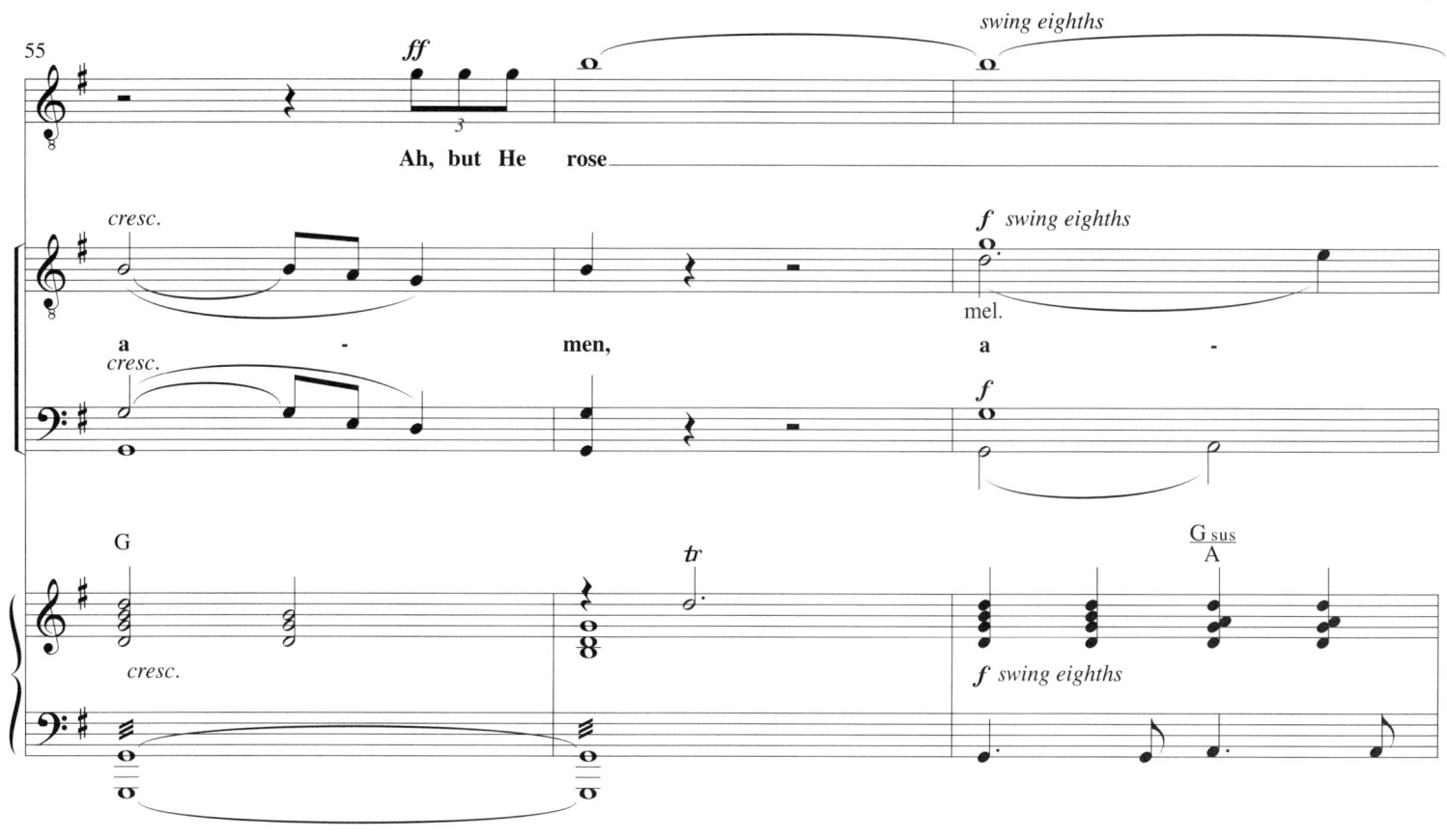

116

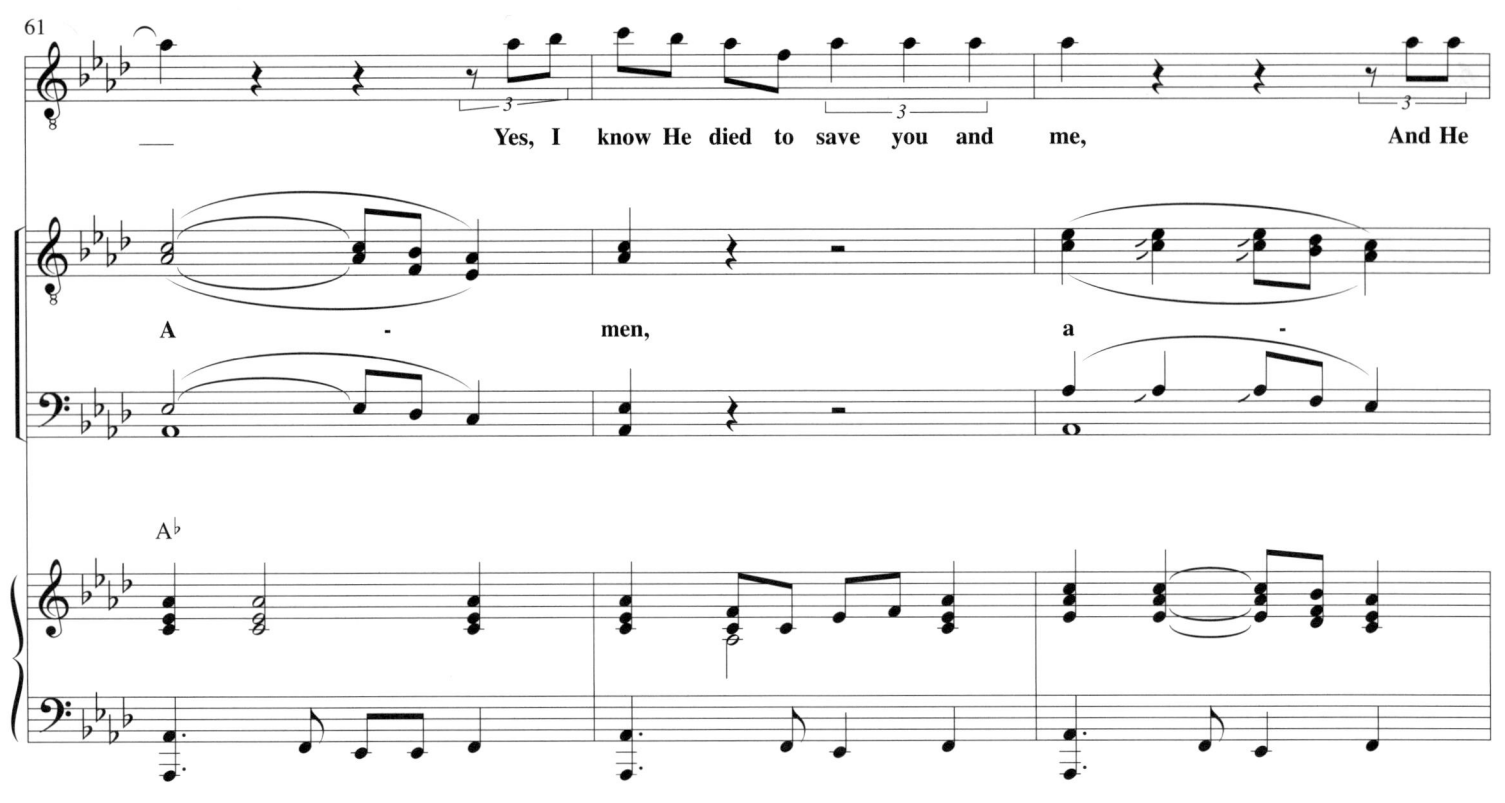

72
rit. poco a poco
straight eighths
And He's com - ing back to take us home.
A - men,
rit. poco a poco
mel.
men, a - men, a -
cresc.
A DM7 A2/C♯ Bm7 A Bm A/C♯ D C♯m7 Bm7 Dm6/F
rit. poco a poco
straight eighths
cresc.

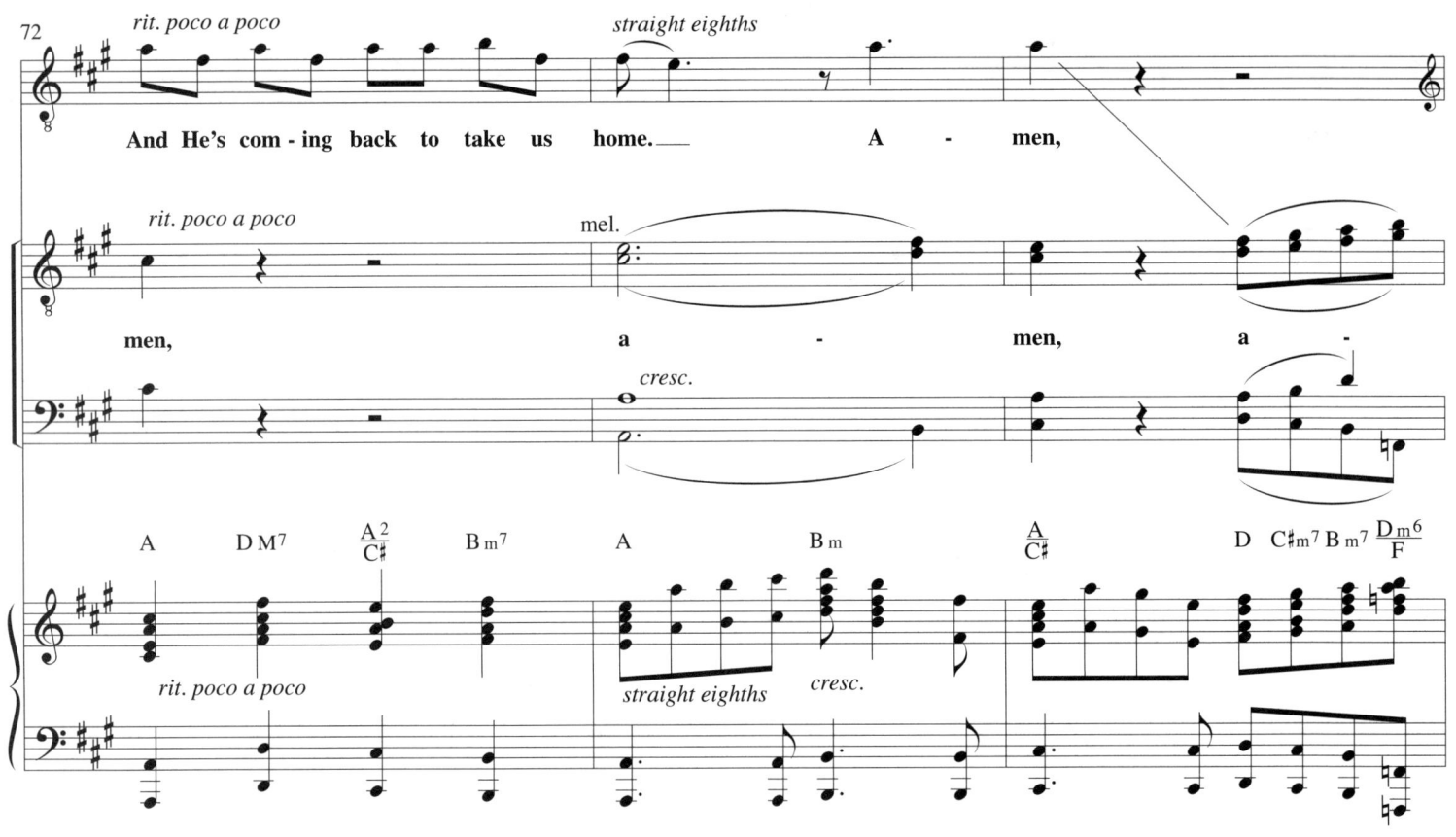

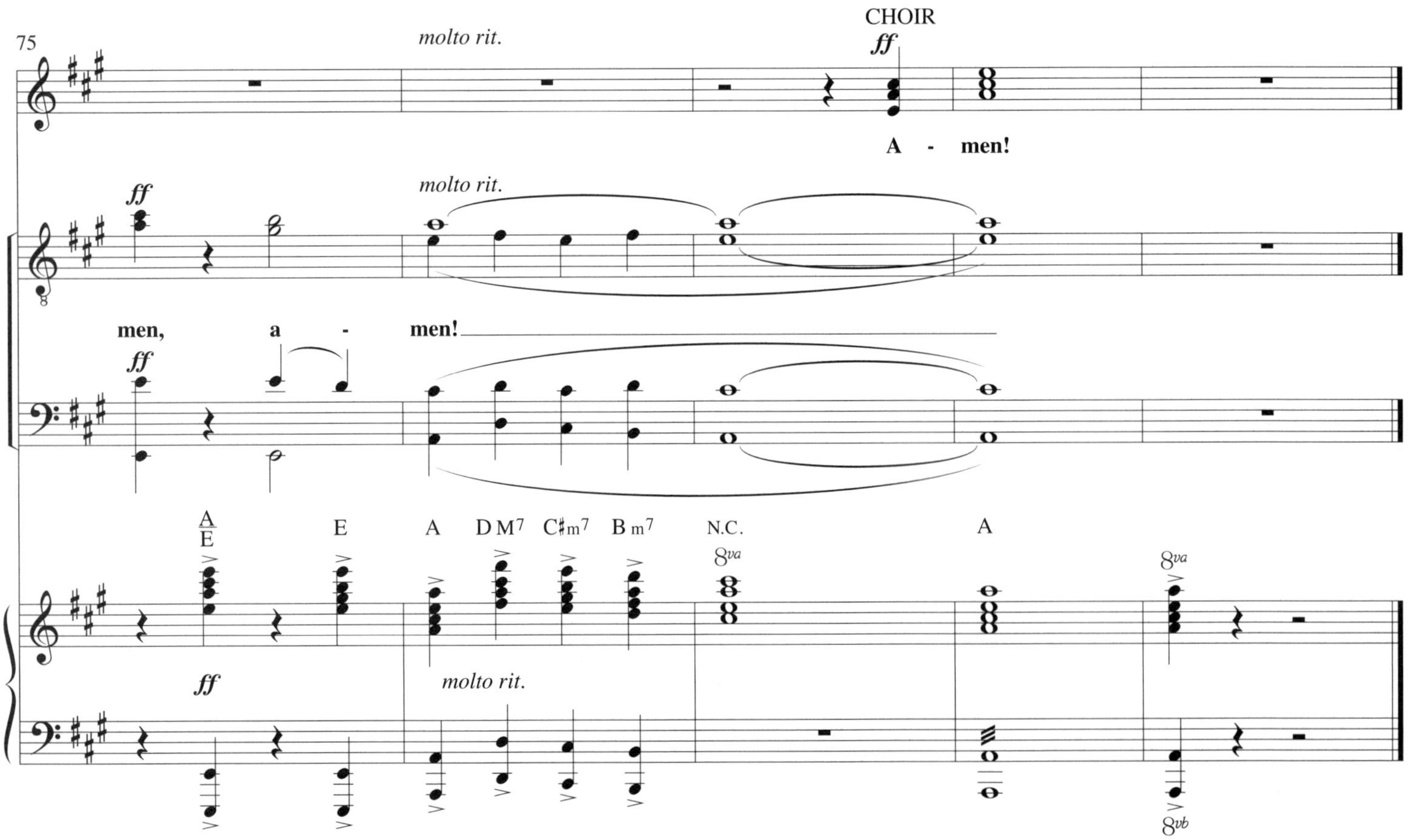
75
molto rit.
CHOIR
ff
A - men!
ff
molto rit.
men, a - men!
ff
A/E E A DM7 C♯m7 Bm7 N.C. A
8va
ff
molto rit.
8vb